Peak District

NORTHERN AND
WESTERN MOORS

Roly Smith
Series editor Andrew Bibby

The Ramblers

FRANCES LINCOLN

The Freedom to Roam guides
are dedicated to the memory of
Benny Rothman

Frances Lincoln Ltd, 4 Torriano Mews, Torriano Avenue, London NW5 2RZ
www.franceslincoln.com

Peak District: Northern and Western Moors
Copyright © Roly Smith 2005

Photographs on pages 12–13, 31, 66–7, 70–71, 112–13 © Ray Manley;
photographs on pages 2, 18–19, 42–3, 49, 56–7, 80–81, 83, 90–91, 98–9,
107, 120–121, 130–31, 137 by Ray Manley © Peak District National Park;
photograph on page 59 © Peak District National Park;
photograph on page 101 © Sheffield Libraries, Archives and Information:
Local Studies; illustration on page 144 © Martin Bagness

Lyrics from 'The Manchester Rambler' song by Ewan MacColl used by kind permission
of Peggy Seeger and of the publisher Harmony Music Ltd

Maps reproduced from Ordnance Survey mapping on behalf of The Controller of Her
Majesty's Stationery Office © Crown Copyright 100043293 2004

First published by Frances Lincoln 2005

British Library Cataloguing in Publication Data
A catalogue record for this book is available from the British Library

ISBN 0-7112-2499-4
Printed and bound in Singapore by Kyodo Printing Co.
9 8 7 6 5 4 3 2 1

Frontispiece photograph: Kinder Downfall

Contents

Acknowledgments

The author would like to express his sincere thanks in particular to Gill Millward, Countryside Access Improvement Officer for Derbyshire County Council, for her vital and most willing help in obtaining copies of the elusive 'conclusive' area maps. Also to Ray Manley for his, as ever, magnificent photography; Mike Rhodes, Access Officer for the Peak District National Park, for checking the routes; Stephen Trotter and Kevin Reid of the National Trust; Rob Morris and Mel Capper at the Countryside Agency and, last but not least, Andrew Bibby for asking me to do the book.

Series introduction

This book, and the companion books in the series, celebrate the arrival in England and Wales of the legal right to walk in open country. The title for the series is borrowed from a phrase much used during the long campaign for this right – Freedom to Roam. For years, it was the dream of many to be able to walk at will across mountain top, moorland and heath, free of the risk of being confronted by a 'Keep Out' sign or being turned back by a gamekeeper.

The sense of frustration that the hills were, in many cases, out of bounds to ordinary people was captured in the song 'The Manchester Rambler' written by one of the best-known figures in Britain's post-war folk revival, Ewan MacColl. The song, which was inspired by the 1932 'mass trespass' on Kinder Scout when walkers from Sheffield and Manchester took to the forbidden Peak District hills, tells the tale of an encounter between a walker, trespassing on open land, and an irate gamekeeper:

He called me a louse, and said 'Think of the grouse',
Well I thought but I still couldn't see
Why old Kinder Scout, and the moors round about
Couldn't take both the poor grouse and me.

The desire, as Ewan MacColl expressed it, was a simple one:

So I'll walk where I will, over mountain and hill
And I'll lie where the bracken is deep,
I belong to the mountains, the clear running fountains
Where the grey rocks rise ragged and steep.

Some who loved the outdoors and campaigned around the time of the Kinder Scout trespass in the 1930s must have thought that the legal right to walk in open country would be won after the Second World War, at the time when the National Parks were being created and the rights-of-way network drawn up. It was not to be. It was another half century before, finally, Parliament passed the Countryside and Rights of Way Act 2000, and the people of England and Wales gained the legal right to take to the hills and the moors. (Scotland has its own traditions and its own legislation.)

We have dedicated this series to the memory of Benny Rothman, one of the leaders of the 1932 Kinder Scout mass trespass who was imprisoned for his part in what was deemed a 'riotous assembly'. Later in his life, Benny Rothman was a familiar figure at rallies called by the Ramblers' Association as once again the issue of access rights came to the fore. But we should pay tribute to all who have campaigned for this goal. Securing greater access to the countryside was one of the principles on which the Ramblers' Association was founded in 1935, and for many ramblers the access legislation represents the achievement of literally a lifetime of campaigning.

So now, at last, we do have freedom to roam. For the first time in several centuries, the open mountains, moors and heaths of England and Wales are legally open for all. We have the protected right to get our boots wet in the peat bogs, to flounder in the tussocks, to blunder and scrabble through the bracken and heather, and to discover countryside which, legally, we had no way of knowing before.

The Freedom to Roam series of books has one aim: to encourage you to explore and grow to love these new areas of the countryside which are now open to us. The right to roam freely – that's surely something to celebrate.

Andrew Bibby, Series editor

Walking in open country – a guide to using this book

If the right and the freedom to roam openly are so important – perceptive readers may be asking – why produce a set of books to tell you where to go?

So a word of explanation about this series. The aim is certainly not to encourage walkers to follow each other ant-like over the hills, sticking rigidly to a pre-determined itinerary. We are not trying to be prescriptive, instructing you on your walk stile by stile or gate by gate. The books are not meant as instruction manuals but we hope that they will be valuable as *guides* – helping you discover areas of the countryside which you haven't legally walked on before, advising you on routes you might want to take and telling you about places of interest on the way.

In areas where it can be tricky to find routes or track down landmarks, we offer more detailed instructions.

Elsewhere, we are deliberately less precise in our directions, allowing you to choose your own path or line to follow. For each walk, however, there is a recommended core route, and this forms the basis on which the distances given are calculated.

There is, then, an assumption that those who use this book will be comfortable with using a map – and that, in practice, means one of the Ordnance Survey's 1:25 000 Explorer series of maps. As well as referring to the maps in this book, it is worth taking the full OS map with you, to give you a wider picture of the countryside that you will be exploring.

Safety in the hills

Those who are already experienced upland walkers will not be surprised if at this point we put in a note on basic safety in the hills. Walkers need to remember that walking in open country, particularly high country, is different from footpath walking across farmland or more gentle countryside. The main risk is of being inadequately prepared for changes in the weather. Even in high summer, hail and even snow are not impossible. Daniel Defoe found this out in August 1724 when he crossed the Pennines from Rochdale, leaving a calm clear day behind to find himself almost lost in a blizzard on the tops.

If rain comes, temperatures will drop, so it is important when taking to the hills to be properly equipped and to guard against hypothermia. Fortunately, walkers today have access to a range of wind- and rain-proof clothing which was not available in the eighteenth century. Conversely, in hot weather, take sufficient water to avoid dehydration and hyperthermia (dangerous overheating of the body).

Be prepared for visibility to drop, when (to use the local term) the clag descends on the hills. It is always sensible to take a compass. If you are unfamiliar with basic compass-and-map work, ask in a local outdoor equipment shop whether they have simple guides available or pick the brains of a more experienced walker.

The other main hazard, even for walkers who know the hills well, is that of suffering an accident such as a broken limb. If you plan to walk alone, it is sensible to let someone know in advance where you will be walking and when you expect to be back – the moorland and mountain rescue services which operate in the areas covered by this book are very experienced but they are not psychic. Groups of walkers should tackle only what the least experienced or least fit member of the party can comfortably achieve. Take particular care if you intend to take children with you to hill country. And take a mobile phone by all means, but don't assume you can rely on it in an emergency, since some parts of the moors and hills will not pick up a signal. (If you can make a call and are in a real emergency situation, ring 999 – it is the police who coordinate mountain and moorland rescues.)

If this all sounds off-putting, that is certainly not the intention. The guiding principle behind the access legislation is that walkers will exercise their new-won rights with responsibility. Taking appropriate safety precautions is simply one aspect of acting responsibly.

Access land – what you can and can't do

The countryside which is covered by access legislation includes mountain, moor, heath, downland and common land. After the passing of the Countryside and Rights of Way Act 2000, a lengthy mapping process was undertaken, culminating in the production of 'conclusive' maps which identify land which is open for access. These maps (although not intended as guides for walking) can be accessed via the Internet, at www.countrysideaccess.gov.uk. Ordnance Survey maps

Note: Each walk has been graded, on a scale of 🥾 to 🥾 🥾 🥾 🥾 🥾, for the degree of difficulty involved. In general, walks are judged more difficult if they are (a) longer in mileage, and/or (b) involve more rough walking (across open moorland rather than on established footpaths), and/or (c) pose more navigational problems or venture into very unfrequented areas. But bear in mind that all the walks in this book require map-reading competence and some experience of hill walking.

published from 2004 onwards also show access land.

You can walk, run, birdwatch and climb on access land, although there is no new right to camp or to bathe in streams or lakes (or, of course, to drive vehicles). Dogs can come too, but the regulations sensibly insist that they are on leads near livestock and during the bird-nesting season (1 March to 31 July). Some grouse moors can ban dogs altogether, so you will need to watch out for local signs.

Access legislation also does not include the right to ride horses or bikes, though in some areas there may be pre-existing agreements which

allow this. More information is available on the website given above and, at the time of writing, there is also an advice line 0845 100 3298.

The access legislation allows for some open country to be permanently excluded from the right to roam. 'Excepted' land includes military land, quarries and areas close to buildings; in addition landowners can apply for other open land to be excluded. For example, at the time of writing, a number of small areas of moorland which are used regularly as rifle ranges have been designated in this way (these are not in areas covered by walks in this book).

Castle Naze

To the best of the authors' knowledge, all the walks in the Freedom to Roam series are either on legal rights of way or across access land included in the official 'conclusive' maps. However, you are asked to bear in mind that the books have been produced right at the start of the new access arrangements, before walkers have begun regularly to walk the hills and before any teething problems on the ground have been ironed out. For instance, at the time of writing there were still some places where entry arrangements to access land had not been finalized. As access becomes better established, it may be that minor changes to the routes suggested in these books will become appropriate or necessary. You are asked to remember that we are encouraging you to be flexible in the way you use the guides.

Walkers in open country also need to be aware that landowners have a further right to suspend or restrict access on their land for up to twenty-eight days a year. (In such cases of temporary closure there will normally still be access on public holidays and on most weekends.) Notice needs to be given in advance, and the plan is that this information should be readily available to walkers, it is hoped at local information centres and libraries but also on the countryside access website and at popular entry points to access land. This sort of arrangement has generally worked well in Scotland, where walkers in areas where deer hunting takes place have been able to find out when and where hunting is happening.

Walkers will understand the sense in briefly closing small areas of open countryside when, for example, shooting is in progress (grouse shooting starts on 12 August) or when heather burning is taking place in spring. However, it is once again too early in the implementation of the access legislation to know how easily walkers in

England and Wales will be able to find out about these temporary access closures. It is also too early to know whether landowners will attempt to abuse this power.

In some circumstances additional restrictions on access can be introduced – for example, on the grounds of nature conservation or heritage conservation, on the advice of English Nature and English Heritage.

Bear these points in mind, but enjoy your walking in the knowledge that any access restrictions should be the exception and not the norm. The Countryside Agency has itself stated that 'restrictions will be kept to a minimum'. If you do find access unexpectedly denied while walking in the areas suggested in this book, please accept the restrictions and follow the advice you are given. However, if you feel that access was wrongly denied, please report your experience to the countryside service of the local authority (or National Park authority, in National Park areas), and to the Ramblers' Association.

Finally, there may be occasions when you choose voluntarily not to exercise your freedom to roam. For example, many of the upland moors featured in these books are the homes of ground-nesting birds such as grouse, curlew, lapwing and pipit, who will be building their nests in spring and early summer. During this time, many people will decide to leave the birds in peace and find other places to walk. Rest assured that you will know if you are approaching an important nesting area – birds are good at telling you that they would like you to go away.

Celebrating the open countryside

Despite these necessary caveats, the message from this series is, we hope, clear. Make the most of the new legal rights we have been given – and enjoy your walking.

Andrew Bibby

15

Introduction

The northern moors of the Peak District were both the cockpit and the catalyst for the freedom to roam movement.

It was on these long-forbidden moors, so close to the teeming populations of the cities of Sheffield and Manchester and the towns of the north Midlands, that the fiercest battles in the fight to obtain the cherished 'right to roam' were fought. It was here that the landowners were most implacable in preserving privacy on their grouse moors and where the pressure was greatest from the factory and mill workers of the surrounding industrial cities, who wanted the right to use the moors for recreation and enjoyment.

With half the population of England living within sixty miles (ninety-five kilometres) of its centre, the Peak District was a convenient playground for literally millions of people – as it still is. But the vast acreage of moorland, which before the enclosure awards of the late eighteenth and early nineteenth centuries had been common land for the use of all, was policed by the owners' strong-arm gamekeepers and strictly forbidden to anyone else. Even local and water authorities enforced 'Keep Out' policies on their moorlands, the water authorities in the interests, so they said, of preventing pollution to the water supplies which fed into the increasing number of reservoirs flooding many of the Dark Peak valleys. Sheep and grouse, apparently, did not pollute the waters like human beings.

In 1934, the writer Phil Barnes estimated that thirty-seven square miles (ninety-six square kilometres) of wild moorland between Manchester and Sheffield were uncrossed even by a public path, and were therefore completely out of bounds to walkers. Kinder Scout, at 2088 ft (636 m) the obvious target for walkers as highest point in the Peak, comprised fifteen square miles (forty square kilometres) without a single public right of way.

Signs sprang up around the edges of the moors warning 'Trespassers Will Be Prosecuted' – which was actually a legal impossibility unless damage was alleged to have been done. The increasingly frustrated ramblers called the signs 'wooden liars' and many quietly continued to practise what the rambling campaigner G.H.B. Ward called 'the gentle art of trespass'.

The most celebrated protest against the exclusion of the public from the moors, the Kinder Scout mass trespass of 24 April 1932, is described in more detail later in the book (see pages 59–60). Vicious prison sentences were passed on five of the trespassers, but their severity rebounded on the authorities and ultimately united the ramblers' cause. (Walk 3 follows the trespassers' route, while Walks 4 and 5 also explore the former 'forbidden mountain' of Kinder Scout.)

Nevertheless it was to be another nineteen years before the Peak District became Britain's first National Park, and the park authority could begin to negotiate access to the northern moors under the powers of the 1949 National Parks and Access to the Countryside Act. Under this legislation, owners were paid an annual amount to allow free access, subject to certain common-sense by-laws. A warden – later ranger – service was set up in 1954, and eventually over eighty square miles (two hundred square kilometres) of moorland were subject to these agreements, including most of the 'battlegrounds' of the 1930s such as Kinder Scout and Bleaklow.

So legal open access is no new phenomenon on many of the northern moors of the Peak District, having been available in some areas for fifty years. The situation on the western moors of the Peak, however, was always more difficult. Even after many years of negotiation between the owners and the Park authority, the glorious heather moorland around the head of the Goyt valley, for example, has not been accessible, apart from by right of way, until now.

The Peak District has often been described as an inland island. It rises proudly from the surrounding plains as the first outpost of highland Britain, a fact which is seen most graphically as you travel at night along one of the pitch-black

moorland roads in the north or west of the National Park, when the street lights of the encircling cities glow below you like a field of stars.

Despite their relatively modest altitude, the hills of the Peak District can create weather conditions which are as severe as anywhere in Britain – especially in winter. There are many tales

The moors above Goyt valley

of walkers underestimating the seriousness of places like Kinder Scout, including Pennine Wayfarers who have turned back, utterly demoralized, only hours after starting out on the first leg across Kinder from Edale. It is worth remembering that the Peak lies on the same latitude as Labrador and Siberia and that a mile on the cloying, glutinous peat of the northern moors is equivalent to about five miles anywhere else, in terms of the amount of energy which has to be expended.

John Derry, in his classic 1926 guidebook *Across the Derbyshire Moors* described such terrain perfectly: 'the most featureless, disconsolate, bog-quaking, ink-oozing moor you ever saw.' Yet these forbidding moors have a large band of *aficionados*, affectionately and accurately known as 'bog-trotters', who perform prodigious feats of mileage across this most unpromising yet challenging of surfaces.

Topographically speaking, the northern and western moors of the Peak District belong to the so-called Dark Park. This is to differentiate them from the softer, more pastoral landscapes of the limestone plateaux and dales of the White Peak to the south. The base rock of the Dark Peak is millstone grit, a coarse, abrasive sandstone which outcrops in the familiar tors of Bleaklow and Kinder (Walks 1–5), the serrated crags of the Roaches and Hen Cloud (Walk 12) and at Shutlingsloe (Walk 11). Beyond the tor-ringed edges, the sombre heather and peat-clad moorlands rise to the highest ground in the National Park at Kinder and Bleaklow.

During the Carboniferous period, about 350 million years ago, the limestone of the White Peak was buried under coarse sediments, grits and mudbanks which spread out in great deltas, like those of today's Mississippi and Nile, from huge rivers flowing from the north. These darker sediments overlaid the limestone in vast quantities, and after aeons of time were solidified into the shale, sandstone and gritstone of the Dark Peak, later to be pushed up into the 'Derbyshire Dome'.

Whereas the limestone was porous and dissolved in water, the gritstone of the Dark Peak was impervious and poorly drained. So any vegetation which grew on the surface, like sphagnum moss, bilberry and heather, quickly rotted down to form immense layers of peat, creating the bleak moorland landscapes of today.

The major rivers of the northern Peak, such as the Derwent, the Ashop and the Noe, exploited the shale valleys which form the border between the limestone and gritstone, and now flow in broad, tree-filled valleys to join the Trent and reach the North Sea. The topography of the western side of the Dark Peak is somewhat more complex and contorted than in the east, and the Goyt and Dane eventually flow into the Mersey and the Irish Sea.

The earliest evidence of human activity in the Peak is the isolated 'microliths' – tiny flakes of flint – which are often found washed out in the peat of the Dark Peak moors, providing a record of the hunting activities of mesolithic (middle Stone Age) man, perhaps 8000 years ago. These were probably seasonal visitors, who only ventured on to the thinly wooded highlands during the summer when conditions were favourable, leaving no trace behind but their stone weapons and implements.

But the high ground of the Dark Peak was obviously important, because this was where, later, the Bronze Age peoples buried their dead leaders. The word 'low' on the OS map in many cases marks a burial mound or tumulus, the word coming from the Old English *hlaw* for hill or burial mound.

The artefacts left behind suggest a relatively high population of simple farmers, and their hut circles and field systems show that they favoured the thin soils of the Dark Peak above the river valley of the Derwent. Archaeologists believe that this area, which is now almost all under rank moorgrass and heather, may have been over-farmed in this period and that this, added to a deterioration in the climate, resulted in succeeding generations moving back to the White Peak area.

The major evidence of the Iron Age in the Peak is found in the so-called hill forts which encircle prominent hills such as Mam Tor above Castleton at the head of the Hope valley (Walk 7) and Castle Naze near Chapel-en-le-Frith (Walk 9). Once thought to be entirely defensive structures, many of these embanked enclosures are now believed to have been used to keep watch over grazing herds of livestock. They were certainly also the meeting places of tribes like the Pecsaetan or 'People of the Peak', and at places like Mam Tor, surely one of the most impressive hill forts in the Pennines, evidence of their hut circles has been found.

The Romans were attracted to the Peak District because of its abundant supplies of lead and it is thought that the forts they left behind, such as Navio at Brough in the Hope valley and Melandra near Glossop, were built to protect these interests. Buxton also had a short-lived fame as a Roman spa, when it was known as Aquae Arnemetiae.

After the Norman Conquest, much of the northern part of the Peak District was commandeered as the Royal Forest of the Peak – a forty-square-mile (hundred-square-kilometre) hunting preserve in which kings and princes pursued game for sport. The forest was administered from William Peveril's castle above Castleton, on the rocky knoll between Peak Cavern and Cave Dale. Macclesfield Forest (Walk 11) was also a hunting preserve dating from the Middle Ages, and was administered by the Earls of Chester.

The great age of rebuilding, which took place in the seventeenth and eighteenth centuries, created mansions like Lyme Park on the edge of Stockport (Walk 8), as wealthy landowners such as the Leghs sought to demonstrate their power and wealth. The formerly open landscape of the Peak was gradually enclosed as these landowners took in more and more land from the moors for cultivation, creating the familiar pattern of dry-stone walls we see today. Chief among the landowners in the north and west were the Earls and later Dukes of Devonshire from Chatsworth, the Dukes of Norfolk, who owned many of the moors around Glossop, and the Earls of Derby, who owned land around the Goyt valley.

After the gradual spread across the Peakland hills of turnpike roads, such as Thomas Telford's Snake Road of 1821 (Walk 2), the railways arrived. Among the earliest constructed in the railway age was the Great Central Railway, which was built through Longdendale in 1847; later came the Midland line in 1866 and the Edale line in 1894.

As the nineteenth century ended, the reservoirs were developed to slake the thirst of the new industrial cities which had sprung up around the edges of the Peak District. Among the first of these were the five which filled the Longdendale valley, and the twin reservoirs of Fernilee and Errwood in the Goyt valley (Walk 10), whose waters went to service the boom towns of Manchester and Stockport.

Pressure for better access was one of the most important influences behind the creation of the Peak District National Park – the first in Britain – in April 1951. Another was the urgent need to conserve the last remaining green space in the south Pennines from unsuitable industrial and residential development. Despite its industrial surroundings, the Peak District had remained a haven for wildlife, and this was a further reason for its designation as a National Park.

The Peak District stands at the crossroads of Britain, at the meeting place of highland and lowland zones. This means that it provides the southernmost habitat for a number of northern species of wildlife, such as the cloudberry and the mountain hare, and the northernmost habitat for some southern species.

The Dark Peak moors support a much less varied wildlife than the dales of the White Peak. The exciting exceptions are the moorland birds of prey, such as the peregrine falcon, the merlin, the goshawk and the hen harrier, all of which are enjoying something of a revival after many years of persecution.

The main agents in the suppression of these magnificent raptors were those same gamekeepers who had tried to force ramblers off the moors in the bad old days. But walkers should never forget that we owe one of the joys of a moorland walk in late summer – the rich tapestry of royal-hued heather – to the gamekeepers who manage these moors almost exclusively for the grouse which their masters delight to shoot after the 'Glorious Twelfth' of August. Heather moorland is the preferred habitat for the red grouse, whose call 'Go back, go back, g'back, g'back' is a constant accompaniment to most walks on the northern and western moors (see pages 83–4).

In the rocky cloughs (steep-sided valleys) of the moorland streams, the clear song of the ring ouzel or mountain blackbird can often be heard, while the spangle-plumed golden plover and curlew are the most common waders seen or heard on the moor tops.

Lyme Park (Walk 8) supports one of the largest and oldest herds of red deer – Britain's largest land mammal – in the Peak. And in the usually snowless winters of these days of global warming, an increasingly common sight on the northern moors is the conspicuous white coat of the mountain hare, which was reintroduced to the area during the nineteenth century for sporting purposes.

Although access has been available on several of the northern moors of the Peak District for many years, they remain the nearest thing to a wilderness in the National Park and a serious challenge to the hillwalker prepared to leave the well-beaten paths. The reward here, as in the comparatively untrodden western moors, is what William Watson in the nineteenth century noted as that 'tremendous silence, older than the world'.

WALK 1

OVER EXPOSED ON BLEAKLOW – BLEAKLOW WEST

DIFFICULTY 👢 👢 👢 👢   **DISTANCE 10 miles (16 km)**

| OLD GLOSSOP | YELLOW-SLACKS | SHELF MOSS | WAIN STONES | BLEAKLOW HEAD | HIGHER SHELF STONES | DOCTOR'S GATE | OLD GLOSSOP |

MAP OS Explorer OL1, The Peak District – Dark Peak area

STARTING POINT Old Glossop (GR 042947)

PARKING In Old Glossop

PUBLIC TRANSPORT Buses from Manchester, Stockport and Buxton to Glossop; trains on the Manchester–Hadfield line

This strenuous moorland ramble takes us to Bleaklow Head, at 2076 ft (633 m) the second-highest summit in the Peak, and also visits perhaps the most interesting of the many aircraft-wreck sites on the Dark Peak moors. This approach to Bleaklow's isolated and wild summit comes from the west, from the old cotton town of Glossop.

■ This walk starts in the oldest part of Glossop, a town whose wealth, like so many of the towns to the west of the Pennines, was founded on the cotton industry. The patronage of

25

the eleventh Duke of Norfolk gave the centre of the town its fine range of civic buildings and squares, and Howardstown, the area of planned early nineteenth-century streets and factories at the western end of the town, still bears the family name. Old Glossop, an unspoilt mixture of old gritstone cottages clustered around the parish church, grew up at the junction of several packhorse routes which crossed the forbidding heights of Bleaklow.

▶ From the centre of Old Glossop, follow Shepley Street, which runs alongside the Shelf Brook, with Shire Hill to the south across to your right. This path leads to a ladder stile and access point on to the open ground of the Lightside ridge, between the unpleasantly named Shittern Clough – apparently it does literally mean 'the clough with a stream used as a sewer' – and the Yellowslacks Brook.

Keep to this ridge, crossing the fence erected by English Nature in 2003 to control sheep grazing on Bleaklow, and climb steadily, bearing right towards the top of the broken rocks of Yellow Slacks ahead ❶. Continue along the edge of these rocks, which culminate in the Dog Rock ❷ above the narrowing confines of Yellowslacks Brook; this changes its name to Dowstone Clough as it flows off the moor in a deep ravine.

■ In 1963 and 1964, during the bad old days of limited access, the rock faces of Yellow Slacks, then known as Bleaklow Bastion, were first tarred and then dynamited by a local farming family in a bid to stop rock climbing there. This happened as the National Park Authority was trying, unsuccessfully, to negotiate an access agreement with the owners. The farmers claimed that the dynamiting was necessary to remove loose stones, which they said were a danger to grazing sheep. An access agreement was eventually finalized and the damage caused in the Sixties is now hardly visible.

▶ Head north-east as you top out on to the moor, in and out of the peat haggs (banks) and groughs (channels) of Shelf Moss towards the beckoning Wain Stones ❸.

■ The isolated Wain Stones were made famous by Alfred Wainwright, who in 1968 in his *Pennine Way Companion*, seems to have been the first to name two of the larges them 'The Kiss'. When seen from a certain angle, and using a little imagination, they can indeed look like the profile of a kissing couple. He famously commented: 'This is the only bit of sex in the book.' Wainwright emphatically did not enjoy Bleaklow (nor Kinder, come to that). He added: 'No one loves Bleaklow. All who get on it are glad to get off.'

▶ It is a short distance north-east from here, following a line of boundary stakes across desert-like peaty ground, to the cairn-topped rocks of the Peak's second-highest summit, Bleaklow Head (2076 ft/633 m).

■ You are now standing on the watershed of England. The 60 in (150 cm) of rain which falls annually on the summit of Bleaklow Head eventually finds its way into either the Irish Sea via the Mersey or the North Sea via the Humber. Despite its considerable elevation, the view from the summit rocks of Bleaklow Head is disappointing. All that can be seen is a barren desert of peat haggs and groughs, with only the chirping of meadow pipits or the occasional cackle of a grouse to break the oppressive silence.

▶ From Bleaklow Head, turn due south passing the Wain Stones again and head for Hern Stones, whose name may come from the Old English *earn*, meaning eagle. Follow the ridge south through a morass of peat groughs, making for the drier ground and scattered rocks and tors of Higher Shelf Stones (GR 089948) ❹. Some of the graffiti on the highest rocks of Higher Shelf Stones is quite old, at least Victorian if the dates are to be believed.

▶ page 30

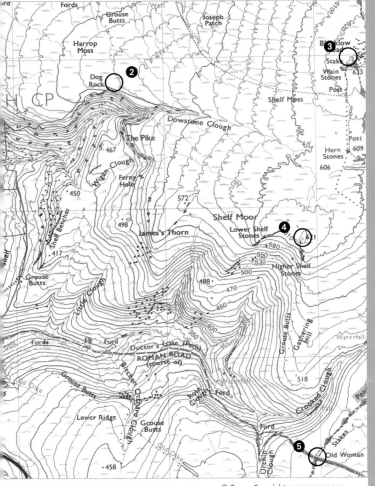

© Crown Copyright 100043293 2004

■ Higher Shelf Stones at 2037 ft (621 m) is one of the finest viewpoints on Bleaklow, and is recognizable to thousands of motorists as the bold northern promontory seen from the summit of Snake Pass (A57), just as it starts to drop down westwards into Glossop. The view extends down the ancient highway of Doctor's Gate and across the deep gash of the Shelf Brook valley. In the foreground is Coldharbour Moor, and the view continues southwards towards the distant Mill Hill and Chinley Churn, with Shining Tor, the highest point in Cheshire, just peeping over the massive northern shoulder of Bleaklow's southern neighbour, Kinder Scout.

Higher Shelf Stones was the scene in 1948 of the tragic crash of a US Air Force B29 Superfortress previously involved in the Berlin Airlift. All thirteen members of the aircrew were killed, and a simple memorial erected on the fortieth anniversary of their deaths now marks the spot. Just beneath the summit to the east there are still large pieces of wreckage including parts of the engines to be seen, and there are stories of ghostly apparitions that have occurred near the spot (see pages 33–4).

The B29 was not the only aircraft to come to grief on this western buttress of Bleaklow. Just to the west of Higher Shelf Stones, on the spur known as James's Thorn, a Canadian Air Force Avro Lancaster bomber crashed soon after VE Day in May 1945, killing all six crew members. And just two months later, a Douglas DC3 Dakota crashed just below Higher Shelf Stones in Ashton Clough, killing the seven airmen on board. Remains of the Dakota can still be seen in the clough.

▶ Descend from Higher Shelf Stones in a south-easterly direction across Gathering Hill – a reference to sheep gathering – following a line of wetter ground marked by rushes, and crossing

Doctor's Gate

Crooked Clough, until you meet the obvious line of the Pennine Way in the deep trench of Devil's Dyke Drain. This is an ancient boundary ditch, possibly dating from the Dark Ages.

After about ½ mile (0.8 km), the Pennine Way becomes a paved highway leading to the Snake Road (A57), but turn right at a place marked Old Woman on the OS map ❺ (possibly a reference to a former standing stone) for the long descent back into Glossop via the ancient causeway that is known as Doctor's Gate.

■ Still marked erroneously on maps as a Roman road, the worn stones on the ancient track of Doctor's Gate are more probably the remnants of a medieval packhorse route. It followed the line of a much older Roman road between the forts of Melandra, now hidden in the vast Gamesley housing estate outside Glossop, and Navio at Brough in the Hope valley. The doctor from whom the route got its name is thought to have been Dr John Talbot, the vicar of Glossop between 1494 and 1550, who apparently was a frequent traveller on this moorland highway.

▶ The route now gradually descends on the obvious Doctor's Gate path, after a short distance crossing English Nature's sheep-excluding fence again and then Urchin Clough (named after long-gone hedgehogs), Rose Clough and Birchin Orchard Clough (presumably named after now vanished fruit trees?). There are superb views across Glossop with its prominent chimney and, further in the distance, towards the tower blocks of Greater Manchester. Shelf Moor and Higher Shelf Stones look down from the right.

The path eventually joins the valley of Shelf Brook, crossing Yellowslacks Brook above Mossy Lea Farm (with its small reservoir one of the largest hill farms in the Peak) ❻. It then contours around tree-topped Shire Hill, with its prominent quarry, to rejoin the outward route and lead back into Old Glossop.

The spooky Superfortress

Stories of phantom aircraft and ghostly airmen are not uncommon around the wreck sites on the Dark Peak moors. But the site where a B29 Superfortress crashed on Higher Shelf Stones, the south-western buttress of Bleaklow, is perhaps the spookiest of all.

In November 1948, the B29 *Over Exposed* was part of the Sixteenth Photographic Reconnaissance Squadron, stationed at the famous former Dambusters' base at RAF Scampton in Lincolnshire. The young crew of *Over Exposed*, led by the fresh-faced thirty-three-year-old Captain Langdon P. Tanner, had completed their service overseas, and were due to return home to the United States in just three days' time.

A routine flight had been scheduled for *Over Exposed* to transport the payroll and some sacks of mail to USAF staff at RAF Burtonwood, near Warrington. It was a mere twenty-five-minute flight, and when Tanner was briefed by Flight Control he was told that he could expect broken clouds at 2000–4000 ft (600–1200 m), with visibility of between four and six miles (six and ten kilometres).

What happened next no one can ever be sure. Maybe Captain Tanner encountered those broken clouds over Bleaklow, and perhaps he nosed down through them to fix his position. Whatever the reason, twenty minutes into the flight *Over Exposed* crashed into the peat hags and groughs just to the north of the 2000-ft (600-m) summit of Higher Shelf Stones. All thirteen crew members were killed either outright or when the aircraft caught fire.

An air search was immediately instigated, and the blazing wreckage of the downed aircraft was spotted by members of the

RAF Mountain Rescue Unit based at Harpur Hill near Buxton. As the rescuers approached from the summit of Snake Pass, they realized that there was nothing they could do to save the crew.

The RAF tried to bury all relics of the crash in the mid-1950s, but there is a surprising amount of the Superfortress still left at the site. The remains include pieces of the four engines as well as fragments of Perspex and twisted steel and aluminium, near a small memorial set up by the people of nearby Glossop, which is always ringed by a group of poppy crosses.

The ghostly story attached to the site comes from the early 1970s. According to David Clarke, in his book *Supernatural Peak District*, a local aviation historian Gerald Scarratt had been at the wreck site during a heavy rainstorm and had uncovered what he thought was a brass washer. When he got home and cleaned the peat from it, he was astonished to find it was a gold wedding ring, inscribed with the name of the captain of the doomed aircraft – Langdon P. Tanner.

Soon after his chilling discovery, he took a party of aircraft wreck enthusiasts to the site to show them where he had made the find. He bent down to point out exactly where he had uncovered the ring, but when he looked up he found that the rest of the party had run off. When he caught up with them, he saw that they were ashen-faced. They said that they had seen someone standing behind and looking down at him – dressed in full flying uniform.

WALK 2

CASTLES IN THE AIR – BLEAKLOW SOUTH

DIFFICULTY  **DISTANCE** 10 miles (16 km)

ALPORT BRIDGE · ALPORT VALLEY · GRAINS-IN-THE-WATER · BLEAKLOW HEAD · ALPORT HEAD · THE RIDGE · BIRCHIN HAT · ALPORT CASTLES · ALPORT BRIDGE

MAP OS Explorer OL1, The Peak District – Dark Peak area

STARTING POINT Alport Bridge, Snake Road (GR 142896)

PARKING Parking at Alport Bridge is limited. There is more space at the lay-by about ½ mile (0.8 km) further north, overlooking Blackden Brook and Kinder Scout.

PUBLIC TRANSPORT Buses from Glossop and Sheffield

The Alport valley has been called the last truly quiet valley in the Peak, and it is indeed one of the few major traffic- and reservoir-free dales in the Dark Peak. Most people will know it for what is claimed to be the largest landslip in the country, the imposing Alport Castles, but what is not so widely known is that it also boasts the finest series of waterfalls anywhere in this generally waterfall-starved region. Accessible only since 2004, the beautiful valley is used as an access route to Bleaklow on this tough moorland walk, during which you may see rare birds of prey.

35

▶ The walk starts from Alport Bridge on the Snake Road (A57), where the River Alport joins the Ashop a little way above the western arm of the Ladybower reservoir. A stile to the side of the bridge allows entry to a footpath which heads uphill to the access track leading northwards through the valley to Alport Castles Farm.

■ This access track was the subject of controversy in 1994, when Forest Enterprise announced plans to harvest and replant the coniferous forestry in the valley above Alport Castles Farm. To do this, they would have had to strengthen and re-engineer the track to make it suitable for 32-ton timber trucks, destroying forever the tranquillity of the valley. A well-attended protest rally was held in August 1996 at the farm, and over 5000 people signed a petition to stop the work. The matter was finally resolved in 2001 when the National Trust acquired the valley and produced, in partnership with

▶ page 40

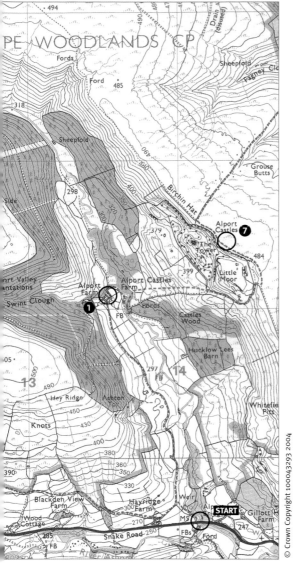

© Crown Copyright 100043293 2004

Map continues northwards on pages 38–9

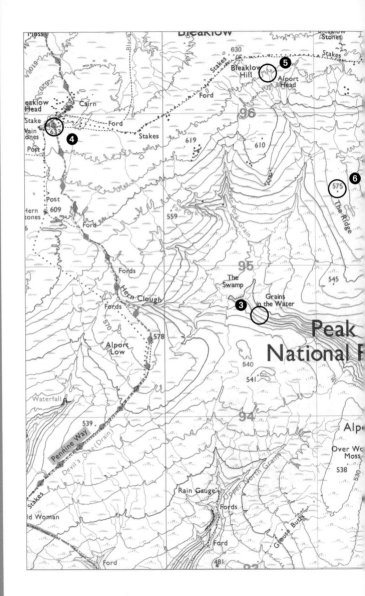

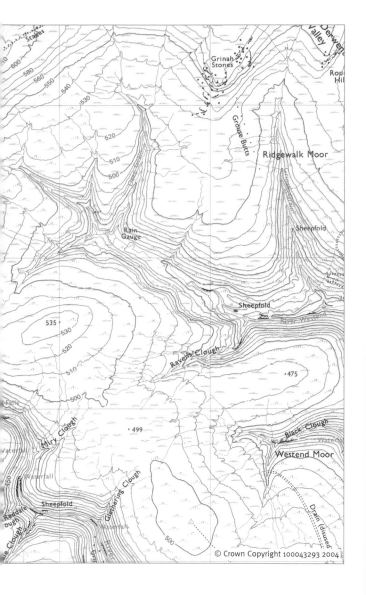

Staves
600
580
560
550
540
530
520
510
500
Grinah Stones
Denver Valley
Rou Hill
Grouse Butts
Ridgewalk Moor
Sheepfold
535
530
520
510
500
Rain Gauge
Sheepfold
River Westend
Ravens Clough
• 475
Fall
Miry Clough
• 499
Black Clough
Waterfa
Waterfall
Westend Moor
Waterfall
Sheepfold
Gathering Clough
Drain (disused)
Reddale ough
Clough
500

the Forestry Commission and others in the Alport Advisory Group, a forty-year strategic plan. This includes the eventual conversion of the coniferous plantations to broad-leaved woodland, the repair of footpaths and the general management of this historic landscape.

▶ The next part of the walk is a pleasant and easy mile (1.6 km) on the track which winds along the western slopes of the Alport, with fine views across the valley towards the minor landslip of Whitefield Pits and, further up, towards Castles Wood plantation. By now the serrated outline of the Alport Castles landslip has appeared ahead on the skyline to the right, and the reason for the romantic name becomes obvious – it does indeed look like the ruined remains of a medieval fortress, dominating the eastern side of the valley. Closer acquaintance with this famous landscape feature will be made on the return route. The track ends at the buildings of Alport Castles Farm ❶, now a private residence in an idyllic setting in the heart of the hills.

■ On the afternoon of the first Sunday of July, the large barn at Alport Castles Farm is the scene of a strange ceremony which many people completely misunderstand because of its title – the Alport Castles Love Feast. But this is no Sixties-style hippy love-in. It is the commemoration, now led by the Methodist Church, of the forty-six clergymen who were persecuted and finally evicted from their parishes on Black Bartholomew's Day in 1662 for standing firm against the newly passed Act of Uniformity. Driven from their livings, they were forced to conduct their now illegal services and 'worship God according to the dictates of their own consciences' in remote spots like the barn at Alport Castles, far from the prying eyes of the authorities. Today's 'Love Feast' is little changed from the seventeenth century, and follows a quiet pattern of hymns and prayers in the unadorned setting of the barn, followed by the 'breaking of the bread' (actually, pieces of cake), which are passed round the congregation in a basket. All then in turn take a drink from a jug of water and after more hymns and prayers those who wish bear testimony to their religious beliefs.

Alport Castles Farm was also the home of Hannah Mitchell, the pioneering suffragette and women's rights campaigner (see pages 46–7).

▶ Passing through the farm buildings, take the faint footpath which leads down to the river and up the valley on its western side, beside the meandering waters of the River Alport and below the controversial forestry plantations away to your left.

■ Some of the dry-stone walls in the valley bottom are quite unlike others in the Peak District, being constructed of large rounded boulders brought down by the river from Bleaklow above. They are thought to be of very ancient origin.

▶ As you get higher up the valley, following a little neck of newly won access land, and cross the river by a long abandoned sheepfold on the edge of the forestry on the eastern bank, the going gets progressively rougher.

Now the first of the Alport's fine series of waterfalls ❷ starts to appear, across from the broken crags of Grindlesgrain Tor on the opposite (western) side of the river. These really are worth the effort of getting close to; some have quite deep plunge pools while others are overhung with ferns and rowan trees, whose scarlet berries in late summer and early autumn make a perfect picture.

The faint path now climbs up the eastern bank, crossing Glethering Clough and turning west as it follows the winding infant river into the very heart of the Bleaklow wilderness. Continuing along the watercourse past another old sheepfold, the next mile (1.6 km) is really hard going, as you cross the well-named Miry Clough and head for the usually boggy bowl known as Grains-in-the-Water ❸.

▶ page 44

The Tower, Alport Castles

■ Grain or grains is a common place name hereabouts, and derives from the Old Norse *grein*, meaning 'a small valley leading off another' – a near-perfect description of the maze of watercourses such as Far Fork and Near Fork Grains which converge on Grains-in-the-Water.

▶ It is now a very rough ½ mile (0.8 km) of bog-trotting (although it will seem like much more) across the notorious ankle-sucking bogs of Bleaklow as you head for the prominent tors of Bleaklow Head ❹ on the skyline due north. At 2076 ft (633 m), this is the high point of the walk, and the second-highest top in the Peak District.

Once you have reached the comparatively drier ground of the Bleaklow summit ridge, turn right following the line of boundary stakes towards Alport Head ❺, which overlooks the source of the river (although this is impossible to identify). Now head due south through the tussocky moorgrass down the pathless and ill-defined

slightly higher ground that is known as The Ridge ❻.

After about a mile (1.6 km) of this, and round about the 545-m spot height on the OS map, turn slightly south-east, keeping to the high ground above the valley of the Alport and the ascent route below to the right. Eventually a path becomes evident and just above Glethering Clough a trig point appears. Continue on the path to Birchin Hat and the jumble of rocks below it, which are Alport Castles ❼.

■ This site is a classic and massive example of a landslip, where a great chunk of gritstone resting on loose and unstable shales has slipped away from the side of the valley to create a scene more like Utah than Derbyshire. Chief among its features is The Tower, a tottering, unstable pinnacle of rock now officially accessible under access legislation but whose summit should really only be attempted by experienced climbers or scramblers. Facing The Tower is the honey-coloured crumbling cliff from which it detached, and a jumbled field of boulders which have fallen from the cliff more recently (and continue to fall, so take care). This is one of the most atmospheric and wild places in the whole of the Peak.

▶ Take some time to explore the wonders of Alport Castles and their southern neighbour, Little Moor, a piece of moorland which has also slipped away from the cliff behind. From the back of Little Moor, a clear path leads down towards the miniscule Alport Castles Farm, backed by the regimented forestry of Swint Clough in the valley below.

Cross the Alport by the footbridge, dedicated to National Trust bird warden Colin Harrod who died in 1994. Climb up back to Alport Castles Farm, to follow the access road and the inward route back to Alport Bridge.

Hannah's legacy

Hannah Mitchell, a hill farmer's daughter from Alport Castles Farm, was many things during her life. She was a suffragette who spent a night in Strangeways prison, a public speaker for the youthful Labour movement, an anti-war campaigner and, later in life, a much-respected councillor for Manchester, who took a particular interest in working-class health and housing issues and in the provision of public libraries.

The erstwhile occupant of a Strangeways cell also became a magistrate. Her autobiography, *The Hard Way Up*, is now considered a classic, though it remained unpublished until after her death. Her story has been used as the basis for displays at the Pumphouse museum of social history in Manchester.

But Hannah Mitchell's childhood was very different from all this. As she put it herself, 'I had been raised in the shadow of Kinder Scout, the wildest part of the Peak of Derbyshire, where winter lasts half the year and the wind blows sear from the hills.' She was born in 1871 and grew up the fourth in a family of six children. Her father was a tenant hill farmer, and life was a struggle. 'My parents had started this farm with borrowed money, which meant a constant struggle to repay,' she wrote. 'Life on those hill-farms at that time was very hard, with no machinery and very little money.'

Her father seems to have been a kindly man, but her mother was deeply unhappy and took her frustration out on her children. In Hannah Mitchell's words, 'The lovely hills and towering rocks which surrounded our home held no beauty for her. They only meant the walls of a prison where her life was unwillingly spent. Her temper was so uncertain that we lived in constant fear of an outbreak which often lasted several days.'

Alport Castles, then as now tucked away in a valley in the hills, was a long way from the nearest school – five miles (eight kilometres) or so, straight across the hills. This meant that the younger children were unable to attend, though Hannah was taught to read by her father and uncle. Eventually, Hannah's turn came to go to school. However: 'It was winter and the journey was too long and rough. The school was badly heated.' Hannah fell ill and had to return home. She had only two weeks' formal schooling in her life.

Hannah Mitchell also recalls the annual religious commemoration known as the Alport Castles Love Feast (see page 40), held each year in her father's barn: 'On Sunday morning we rose early, for by nine o'clock the worshippers began to arrive, mostly on foot, as the big coaches from the distant towns had to be left at the end of the narrow lane. Groups of twenty or thirty arriving in this isolated spot seemed a multitude to us, who rarely saw a stranger from one year's end to the next.'

Perhaps this annual influx of strangers encouraged her to make her own move away from rural life. She went to Glossop, initially into service. Then she moved to Bolton, to Ashton-under-Lyne and finally to north Manchester. She became caught up in the political and social ferment of that time, and played an active part in the campaigns of the suffragette movement which were centred on the Pankhursts in Manchester, including, on one occasion, heckling Winston Churchill who was then a leading Liberal politician.

Hannah Mitchell has no plaque or memorial at Alport Castles to record her childhood in the Peak District, but she has left behind the record of her life in her book. As she wrote: 'Life to me has been a great adventure, a wonderful thing rounding itself off with time to sit back and rest. The work we began, the cause we sponsored, the faith we held will all remain to be carried on, we hope, by abler hands than ours.'

Sheep that *don't* go astray

Whitefaced Woodlands sheep are a rare breed which originate from the Woodlands valley, which runs up from the Ladybower reservoir to the Snake Pass between Kinder Scout and Bleaklow.

They are one of the largest of British hill breeds of sheep, with a white face and legs and a long Roman nose with pinkish nostrils. They have long tails and both rams and ewes sport horns, the rams' being unusually heavy and spiralled. In the eighteenth century, the Duke of Devonshire is said to have tried to improve the native breeds kept by his tenants on the Snake Pass, importing Merino rams from the royal flocks at Kew. This is perhaps what has given the Whitefaced Woodlands their very fine, long-stapled wool. They are also known as Penistone sheep, named after the West Yorkshire market town on the edge of the Peak where they were also very popular.

There are still a few local keepers of this ancient breed, notably the Shirt family of Edale, and a local saying is still: 'As wild as a Woodland tup [ram].'

Like many other breeds of moorland sheep, Woodlands are known for their strong 'hefting' instinct, that is their attachment to the wild and windswept moors where they were born and which are their home. There is a story that a pair of Woodland rams were sold from Rowlee Farm on the Snake Road in the nineteenth century to a farmer in Kent. They could not settle in their new lowland home in the Garden of England, and escaped and eventually found their way back nearly 200 miles (320 km) across country to their home pastures in the Woodlands valley.

The mounted head of one of these adventurous sheep was rescued from a local pub and can be seen in the Boyd Dawkins Room at the Buxton Museum and Art Gallery.

Whitefaced Woodlands sheep

WALK 3

STEPPING OUT WITH THE TRESPASSERS – KINDER WEST

DIFFICULTY 👢 👢 👢 👢   **DISTANCE 8 miles (13 km)**

BOWDEN BRIDGE, HAYFIELD	KINDER RESERVOIR	WILLIAM CLOUGH	ASHOP HEAD	KINDER DOWNFALL	TUNSTEAD CLOUGH FARM	BOWDEN BRIDGE

MAP OS Explorer OL1, The Peak District – Dark Peak area

STARTING POINT Bowden Bridge, Hayfield (GR 048869)

PARKING Bowden Bridge National Park car park

PUBLIC TRANSPORT Half-hourly buses run from Stockport, Glossop and New Mills to Hayfield, linking to the Buxton–Stockport train service.

Three-quarters of a century ago, Hayfield was the starting point for the Battle of Kinder Scout. This serious moorland walk follows in the footsteps of the 1932 trespassers, and visits some of the places forbidden to them, such as Kinder Low, 2077 ft (633 m), and Kinder Downfall, the highest waterfall in the Peak.

■ A bronze plaque in the wall of Bowden Bridge quarry states that the mass trespass on Kinder Scout started here on 24 April 1932 (see pages 59–60). About 400 ramblers gathered and set off along the route we will follow.

▶ Turn left out of the quarry and follow the undulating Kinder Road, branching off right after about ½ mile (0.8 km) by a footpath sign near the gates of the water works. Crossing the river, turn almost immediately left through a gate on to a broad riverside path. Eventually cross the river again by a footbridge below the grassy dam of the Kinder reservoir, which was constructed in the early years of the twentieth century.

Go through the symbolic 'Access to Open Country' gate on the right, which is also signposted White Brow, and follow the steep, expertly pitched path which climbs, a wall to the right, up the slopes of White Brow ❶. The path degenerates to a rocky and at times boggy footpath. Follow it through a gate and then around Nab Brow.

■ This is a glorious promenade along the lower slopes of Leygatehead Moor, with fine views across the sparkling waters of the Kinder reservoir towards the objective, the distant cleft of Kinder Downfall, seen on the skyline ahead.

▶ The path eventually descends by a pretty cascade into William Clough ❷, which is said to have been named after a medieval metal-worker who had a smelting works here. Turn left before the footbridge to follow the (signed) Snake Path – a right of way since 1897 – up beside the clough and into its narrowing confines.

Alternatively, you can cross the footbridge to head north-east across Hollin Head for a direct ascent of Sandy Heys, cutting out William Clough and Ashop Head and joining the perimeter path to Kinder Downfall there.

The rough, rocky path up William Clough rises steeply, crossing and re-crossing the stream or winding high on its banks, passing the point where the 1932 trespass actually took place. After a steady ascent through a canyon-like section, it emerges to what used to be a tricky, badly eroded section of shale near the top, but which is now a restored slabbed stairway.

▶ page 54

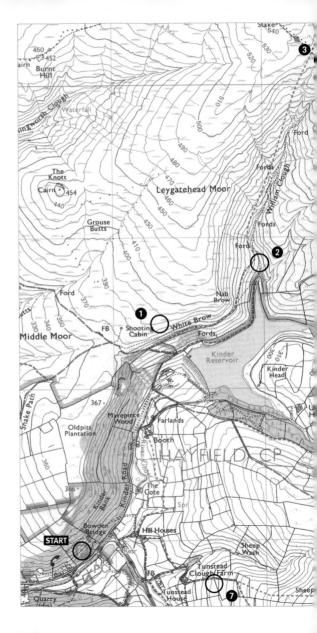

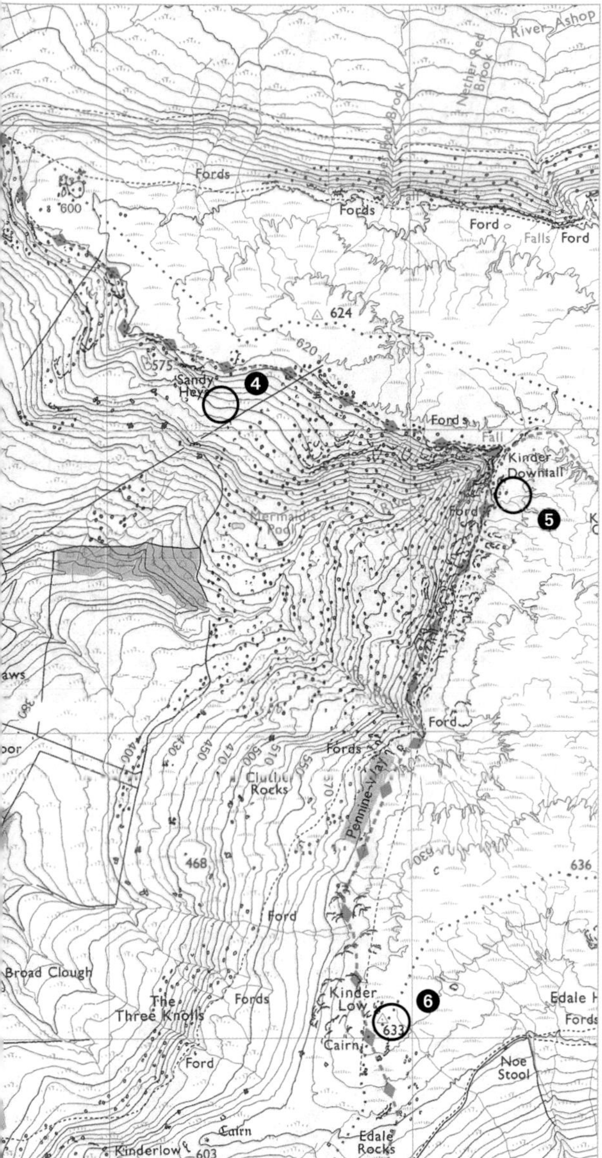
River Ashop
Nether Red Brook
Brook
Fords
600
Fords
Ford
Falls
Ford
624
620
575
Sandy Heys
4
Fords
Fall
Kinder Downfall
Ford
5
Mermaid's Pool
Ford
Fords
Pennine Way
Cluther Rocks
400
430
450
470
500
510
550
570
630
636
468
Ford
Broad Clough
The Three Knolls
Fords
Kinder Low
6
633
Cairn
Fords
Noe Stool
Ford
Cairn
Kinderlow Cavern
603
Edale Rocks

About 20 yards (20 m) from the top of William Clough, a flagged path leads off to the right towards the prominent escarpment of Ashop Head ❸, the westernmost buttress of Kinder, which towers ahead to the right. Ashop Head is a major crossroads of the footpaths to the west of Kinder including the Pennine Way.

■ The beautifully constructed natural stone-set pitched path which leads up to Ashop Head is an award-winning example of unobtrusive footpath restoration. The work was carried out by the National Trust's High Peak Estate, working with the National Park Authority and the Countryside Agency, which is responsible for the Pennine Way National Trail.

The Pennine Way, which runs 270 miles (435 km) from Edale to Kirk Yetholm, opened in 1965, the brainchild of access campaigner Tom Stephenson (see pages 74–5). Today it is still one of Britain's most popular long-distance footpaths but with its popularity have come severe

problems of erosion, especially in soft peat country like Kinder, Bleaklow and Black Hill – hence the need for the kind of remedial work seen at Ashop Head.

▶ Turn right at the top near a large cairn and follow the edge path below Mill Hill Rocks towards the next prominent headland of Sandy Heys, the north-westernern bastion of Kinder Scout, which is about ½ mile (0.8 km) of rough walking ahead ❹. (The alternative route suggested above meets up with the route here.)

Still following the line of the Pennine Way, which keeps to easier walking on the edge of the plateau, the path passes between flat, rocky outcrops with glimpses of the glinting, watery eye of the Mermaid's Pool on the boulder-strewn moor beneath.

■ This dark, reedy little mountain tarn has many legends attached to it. Local people used to believe that if you visited the pool on the eve of Easter Day, you would see a beautiful mermaid and thus be granted the gift of eternal life. Before you scoff at the idea, one nineteenth-century Hayfield resident, Aaron Ashton, was a frequent visitor to the pool and he lived to the ripe old age of 104 (see page 61).

▶ Continue on the path towards the increasingly impressive rocky amphitheatre of Kinder Downfall ❺, reached by passing through more weird, wind-eroded tors.

■ This 100-ft (30-m) waterfall is the highest in the Peak District, and one of the first landmarks on the Pennine Way. The Kinder river drops off the plateau here but be warned, in summer it is never much more than a disappointing trickle. In wet weather, however, the Downfall is impressive, especially when a westerly wind funnels up the valley and blows back the water as a shifting curtain hanging in the air. This is one of the best-known spectacles of the Peak, and in the right conditions it can be seen as far away as Stockport. Only rarely in winter these days is the waterfall transformed into a shimmering wall of ice, attracting climbers to one of the few ice-climbing opportunities in the Peak.

The Downfall is probably the feature which gave the entire mountain its name. On old maps, the area around the Downfall is known as Kinder Scout, and the name, which may originally be Norse, has been translated as 'water falling over the edge', which is a pretty accurate description. The Downfall is the Piccadilly Circus of Kinder, a popular lunchspot which also attracts a scruffy band of voracious sheep who are not above pinching walkers' sandwiches.

▶ Turn south from the Downfall following the well-trodden line of the Pennine Way as it swings around the chasm of Red Brook, which neatly frames the Mermaid's Pool, and then across much drier and firmer ground towards the beckoning white trig point of Kinder Low ❻.

▶ page 58

William Clough

■ Kinder Low at 2077 ft (633 m) is only 11 ft (3 m) lower than the actual summit of Kinder Scout – and a lot easier to find. It is situated in a desert-like expanse of wind-blown peat and sand, the result of years of over-grazing, moorland fires, and wind and acid-rain erosion. John Hillaby must have been thinking of Kinder Low when he described the Kinder moors in his *Journey through Britain* as, in botanical terms, 'an example of land at the end of its tether. All the life has been drained off or burnt out, leaving behind only acid peat. You can find nothing like them anywhere else in Europe.'

▶ As you are now in open country, you can cut down due west across the open moor from Kinder Low to the prominent triple rocks of the Three Knolls, heading south-west beneath Kinderlow End to join the path which comes up from Tunstead

Clough Farm. This leads down to the intake wall and access point.

■ Marked on the map to the east of Kinderlow End is 'Kinderlow Cavern', but you will search in vain to find it. According to Luke Garside writing in 1880 in *Kinder Scout: The Footpaths and Bridleways about Hayfield*: 'Although several inflated descriptions have been given of this cavern "as running through the bowels of the mountain," Etc, we may say that it is merely a huge circuitous hole, not worth notice by those who may have visited the caverns in Castleton and near Buxton.' Even Garside's 'circuitous hole' was filled in by the landowner many years ago, in order to stop too many curious visitors.

▶ Go around Tunstead Clough Farm ❼ by passing through a series of kissing gates, and then walk easily down its access road to Bowden Bridge and back to the car park.

Forgive us
our trespassers

In April 1932 Kinder Scout, at 2088 ft (636 m) the summit of
the Peak District, was a forbidden mountain for ramblers,
strictly preserved by grouse-shooting landowners and their
gamekeepers. A group of members of the communist-inspired
British Workers' Sports Federation, led by an unemployed
mechanic called Benny Rothman, had been turned off Bleaklow
a few weeks before by some intimidating landowners. The
Manchester-based group were frustrated by the lack of progress
being made through negotiation by the official Ramblers'
federations towards the establishment of National Parks and the
right to roam, and so they decided to take direct action.

In a well-publicized event, they advertised the fact that
they would deliberately trespass on Kinder Scout to call the

Participants in the 1932 Kinder mass trespass

owners' bluff, and around 400 of them gathered in Bowden Bridge quarry, Hayfield, on the bright sunny Sunday morning of 24 April 1932. After Rothman had been pressed into addressing the crowd from a ledge in the quarry they set off, singing cheerfully, for Kinder.

At a pre-arranged signal as they ascended William Clough, they broke ranks and swarmed up the open moor below Sandy Heys, where they were met by a small force of gamekeepers. In the ensuing mêlée one gamekeeper was slightly injured, and several ramblers were arrested when they returned to Hayfield. Five of them later received prison sentences at Derby Assizes of up to six months for riotous assembly, but their point had been made.

The severity of the sentences handed down by the judge had the unexpected effect of uniting the rambling fraternity, and ensured that when the Peak District National Park was finally designated in 1951 one of the first actions the park authority took was to negotiate access agreements with the landowners of Kinder Scout and Bleaklow.

Today the trespassers' dreams have been realized, and the right of freedom to roam in all open country is now enshrined in law through the Countryside and Rights of Way Act 2000.

The mermaid's tale

Although just about as far from the sea as you can get in Britain, Mermaid's Pool is the name given to the small reed-fringed lake on a plateau beneath the western escarpment of Kinder Scout, in the valley of the Kinder River below the Downfall.

A couple of other peaty tarns over on the Staffordshire side of the Peak also have associations with mermaids. Doxey Pool (see pages 137–8) lies on the Roaches in the Staffordshire moorlands, and has an evil reputation involving an unpleasant spirit known as Jenny Greenteeth, while the circular pool called Blake Mere can be found close to the Mermaid Inn high on the Staffordshire moors east of Leek, and is thought to be bottomless.

The legend of Kinder's Mermaid's Pool is that it is used by a beautiful, long-haired mermaid who lives in a cave close by and comes down to bathe there once a year on the eve of Easter Day. If you are fortunate enough to see this beautiful vision, it is said, you will be granted eternal life.

There are tales of men from the nearby village of Hayfield who became fascinated by the story, and presumably by the prospect of everlasting life. One is said to have caught a glimpse of her and to have been taken into her cave, never to be seen again. The other, better-documented story is of Aaron Ashton, a retired soldier from Hayfield who at the turn of the last century regularly made the Easter Eve pilgrimage to the tarn in order to see the mermaid. He never said, however, if he saw her, but the fact is that he lived to the ripe old age of 104, dying in 1835.

The author's most memorable trip to the Mermaid's Pool was during the bitter winter of 1977–8, when he trudged up to witness the now rare sight of Kinder Downfall frozen into a hundred-foot sparkling chandelier of ice. Mermaid's Pool was also frozen over, and by its side someone had built a complete and perfect igloo.

WALK 4

KINDER SUMMIT AND THE WOOL PACKS – KINDER SOUTH

DIFFICULTY 👢 👢 👢 👢   **DISTANCE About 7 miles (11 km)**

UPPER BOOTH — CROWDEN BROOK — WOOL PACKS — KINDER SUMMIT — EDALE ROCKS — JACOB'S LADDER — UPPER BOOTH

MAP OS Explorer OL1, The Peak District – Dark Peak area

STARTING POINT Upper Booth

PARKING In large lay-by just under the railway bridge past Whitmore Lea Farm, Barber Booth (GR 108847)

PUBLIC TRANSPORT Edale village (Grindsbrook Booth) is served by trains from Stockport and Sheffield.

Once threatened by the construction of a steel works, the Edale valley, standing in the shadow of the Peak's highest hill, Kinder Scout, is now a firm favourite for Dark Peak walkers. This exploration of the southern edges of Kinder ascends to the summit by one of the less frequented routes and also takes in some of the most striking and unusual rock formations, descending by one of the ancient packhorse routes which cross the mountain.

▶ From the lay-by, continue up the minor road which leads towards the dale head and soon descends into the neat, National Trust-owned hamlet of Upper Booth ❶. The first farm usually does teas for walkers during the season.

■ The Edale valley is marked by a series of small hamlets all of which have the suffix 'booth'. Booth comes from an Old Danish word meaning a temporary shelter used by stockmen, and Edale has five. From the head of the valley they are: Upper Booth, Barber Booth, Grindsbrook Booth (now usually known as Edale village), Ollerbrook Booth and Nether Booth.

▶ Take the footpath which leads right just after crossing the bridge over the River Noe in Upper Booth, and ascend on a narrow path through the trees alongside Crowden Brook. The path keeps just below the wall and heads almost due north towards the encircling hills.

Cross a delightful wooden footbridge in a rowan-shaded hollow and ascend the opposite bank of the clough which, with its interlocking spurs, now assumes the character of a Highland glen. The path winds easily up the clough before descending to the stream as the valley narrows.

The great buttress of the rock known as Crowden Tower, looking like the keep of a great medieval castle, now appears on the skyline to the left. As the valley narrows still further choose the best route you can, scrambling over boulders and constantly crossing the stream. The easiest route is slightly up the grassy hillside to the left.

After an entertaining little scramble up the final rocks under the tower – not so easy when ice-encrusted in winter – you emerge on to the featureless plateau of Kinder Scout.

■ John Hillaby, in his book *Journey through Britain,* memorably described the top of Kinder Scout as looking as if 'entirely covered in the droppings of dinosaurs'. Kinder is a 15-sq-mile (40-sq-km) morass of peat bogs, haggs and groughs, which constitutes the highest point of the Peak District. It is also the highest ground in England south of the Yorkshire Dales, and is said to amount to the greatest area of land in England above 2000 ft (610 m). It is still misleadingly marked on some maps as 'The Peak', but anything less like the 'sharply pointed hill' of the dictionary definition would be difficult to find.

▶ Turn left and scramble up the rocks to admire the view from the top of Crowden Tower (2030 ft/ 619 m) ❷, which extends down the steep-sided Crowden Clough towards the long, gulley-scored line of Rushup Edge across the trench of Edale to the south.

Take the broad perimeter path which leads between banks of peat towards the next objective, the curious collection of rocks known as the Wool Packs ❸.

■ There are several alternative names for these extraordinary tors but the original one of the Wool Packs

▶ page 68

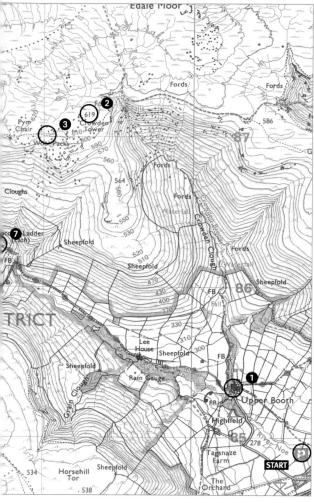

Edale Moor

Fords

Fords

619
Crowden Tower

Pym Chair

Woolpacks

586

587

Fords

Fords

Waterfall

Crowden Clough

564

Cloughs

Ladder (Path)

FB

Sheepfold

Sheepfold

Fords

Waterfall

Sheepfold

FB

86

Fall

Sheepfold

TRICT

Lee House

Sheepfold

FB

Sheepfold

330
310
300

Grain Clough

Rain Gauge

FB

Upper Booth

Highfield

River Noe

85

278

Tagsnaze Farm

START

534

Horsehill Tor

538

Sheepfold

The Orchard

N

© Crown Copyright 100043293 2004

The Wool Packs, Kinder Scout

came about through their resemblance to the bulging packs of wool carried by packhorse trains. Some individual tors also have their own names. These include the Moat Stone, which is often surrounded by water, the Anvil, the Pagoda and the huge throne-like Pym Chair, perhaps named after the Puritan leader, John Pym (see page 73).

▶ After exploring the Wool Packs, it's time to do some real bog-trotting if you want to reach the elusive actual summit of Kinder Scout (2088 ft/636 m, GR 085875) ❹. You need to head due north-west from Crowden Tower, crossing a maze of haggs and groughs for about ½ mile (0.8 km) to reach Point 636 (as it is known), which is usually marked by a small cairn of stones and a stake. You need to be a real die-hard summit-bagger to reach Kinder's summit, for there's not much to see there other than peat.

Returning to the perimeter track, after passing the giant anvil of Noe Stool ❺ (Kinder is known on the earliest maps as 'Now

Stoole Hill'), the path becomes a raised causeway across some very boggy ground as you approach the hill known as Swine's Back, below Edale Rocks. The path swings down below the escarpment to join the Pennine Way at a crossroads of paths near Edale Cross (Edale Cross itself is away to the right) ❻.

■ Edale Cross is an ancient boundary marker which has guided the way for countless generations of travellers crossing the western shoulder of Kinder Scout. It may have originally been erected as early as the twelfth century to define the lands of Basingwerk Abbey in north Wales, and it stood at the exact centre of the medieval Royal Forest of the Peak, where the forest's three wards met. It bears the date mark of 1610, but was re-erected by local farmers in 1810 (the initials 'JG' refer to one of them, John Gee). The cross has now been enclosed in a rather incongruous three-sided wall by its latest owners, the National Trust.

▶ From the crossroads, follow the Pennine Way due east to the head of Jacob's Ladder ❼, the top of which has also gained some unsightly flat-topped low urban walling in recent years.

■ This famous route climbing out of the head of the Edale valley is said to have been constructed by Jacob Marshall, a seventeenth-century packhorse trader of Edale Head House, which now lies in ruins above and to the right of the route. Marshall made this shortcut up the hillside for himself, while his laden pony took the longer, zigzag route, which can still be made out over to the right. The route was reconstructed by the National Trust in the late 1980s using stone pitching after it had suffered serious erosion. It now forms part of the re-aligned Pennine Way.

▶ The pretty little packhorse bridge which crosses the River Noe at the foot of Jacob's Ladder is known as Yongate Bridge. It is now an easy stroll along the track leading down past Lee Farm to Upper Booth, with Brown Knoll, cut by the ravine of Grain Clough, across the valley of the Noe to your right.

Southern slopes of Kinder, with Swine's Back in the background

The grand tors

The weird shapes of the gritstone tors which ring the Kinder Scout plateau and which are found on the highest points of Bleaklow are among the most abiding memories of walking on the Dark Peak moors. Their strange, other-worldly silhouettes and odd names enliven many a moorland walk, but how were they formed and where did they get those evocative names?

Tors – it's an Old English name which means 'rock, rocky outcrop or hill' – are the result of aeons of weathering by the triple agents of water, ice and wind. Tors are thought to be the surviving cores of a much larger mass of sandstone rock which once covered the area but which has gradually been eroded away around them. Another theory is that they are the remaining blocks of a landslipped area which slumped away under periglacial (edge-of-ice-sheet) conditions.

The distinctive shapes of the tors are created by erosion. Slightly acidic rainwater eats into the rock joints, and frost and ice carry on the process as water in the joints freezes and expands. The effects of wind-blasting are perhaps less obvious, but at the end of the last Ice Age, around 12000 years ago, there was much less vegetation cover and rock particles eroded from the surface were blown far and wide by the Arctic gales. It was this wind-blasting which provided the final smoothly rounded shapes of the upstanding tors.

These isolated rocks can assume some odd shapes, such as the weird collection on the southern slopes of Kinder Scout which are known as the Wool Packs from their resemblance to the rounded packs of wool carried by packhorse trains. The alternative names for the Wool Packs reflect their animalistic and natural shapes, for they are also known among walkers and climbers as Whipsnade and the Mushroom Garden.

Near by is the anvil-shaped Noe Stool, named after the river which flows through Edale and which rises just below Pym Chair (a chair-shaped outcrop thought to take its name from the seventeenth-century Nonconformist preacher John Pym) and the Pagoda (named for its resemblance to a Chinese temple). Another tor with an Oriental connection is the Chinese Wall on Seal Edge. This outcrop, and the Boxing Glove Stones on the Edge, are both on the northern escarpment of Kinder.

The stories behind Madwoman's Stones on Kinder's eastern side and Ringing Roger above Edale are unknown, although the name of Ringing Roger is probably derived from the French *roches* for rocks, and the outcrop is also known locally as Echoing Rock.

Across the Snake Pass on Bleaklow, the Peak's second-highest summit has its own collection of eccentric tors, many of which, like Noe Stool, seem to have been carved by the wind into anvil shapes. The Anvil Stone itself and the three-pronged Trident are both at Bleaklow Stones. Grinah Stones, another collection of tors on the eastern edge of Bleaklow's summit, are curiously pock-marked, like Gruyère cheese. As mentioned above (page 27), the Wain Stones near by can from a certain angle look like a couple about to kiss.

The strange shapes of the tors are said to have influenced the work of Yorkshire's world-famous sculptor, Henry Moore, and if you compare photographs of his works with some of the Pennine tors you can clearly see how the connection was made.

He did it his Way

In June 1935 Tom Stephenson, the open-air correspondent of the *Daily Herald*, received a letter from two young American girls who were planning to come to England for a walking holiday. When they asked if there was anything in England similar to their long-distance Appalachian Trail, it set him thinking.

The paper was short of a centre-page feature at the time, so Tom eagerly filled it by working out a possible route for the girls. 'Why should we not press for something akin to the Appalachian Trail – a Pennine Way from the Peak to the Cheviots?' Tom asked in the now famous feature which carried the headline: 'Wanted – a Long Green Trail'.

'This need be no Euclidean line,' he explained, 'but a meandering way deviating as needs be to include the best of that long range of moor and fell; no concrete or asphalt track, but just a faint line on the Ordnance Maps which the feet of grateful pilgrims would, with the passing years, engrave on the face of the land.'

Tom Stephenson was a great campaigner for access to mountain and moorland, and his hidden agenda behind the idea of the Pennine Way was to crack the problem of providing access to the then 'forbidden mountains' of Kinder and Bleaklow. Half of the missing rights of way which needed to be negotiated for his new route – which started from Edale in the Peak and led through the highest parts of the Pennines to the Cheviots and the Scottish Border – were in this section. Tom was keeping a dossier of incidents which had already occurred between ramblers and gamekeepers.

It was to take another thirty years of hard negotiation for Tom's dream to become a reality, by which time his career had moved on, as he became first Press Officer to the Ministry of Town and Country Planning and then Secretary of the Ramblers' Association, a post he held for twenty-one years.

But eventually, on 24 April 1965, hundreds of ramblers gathered on Malham Moor to celebrate the long-awaited opening of the 270-mile (435-km) Pennine Way – Britain's first and toughest long-distance footpath. Tom's dream of a 'Long Green Trail' had at last been realized.

Since then, of course, the Pennine Way has seen its fair share of problems, and Tom's 'faint line on the Ordnance Maps' soon became a footpath motorway in some places. Path erosion, especially in the soft-peat sections such as Kinder, Bleaklow and Black Hill, became a real concern. The Peak District National Park had a full-time maintenance team working exclusively on the first forty miles (sixty-four kilometres) of the route for several years, and some of the techniques they introduced have been copied in other places where erosion has become a problem.

Careful pitching of stones on steep sections, such as at Ashop Head on Kinder, and the re-use of gritstone paving slabs from derelict mills, which were 'floated' on a geo-textile mat in boggy places such as on Kinder and Bleaklow, were pioneering footpath-restoration techniques, ironically utilizing technology introduced by the Romans. In some places, while not exactly a 'concrete or asphalt track', Tom Stephenson's long green trail had become a victim of its own success.

WALK 5

KINDER'S NORTHERN EDGES

DIFFICULTY 👟 👟 👟 👟

DISTANCE About 10 miles (16 km)

| SNAKE INN | SEAL EDGE | FAIR BROOK RAVINE | FAIRBROOK NAZE | THE EDGE | ASHOP HEAD | SNAKE PATH | SNAKE INN |

MAP OS Explorer OL1, The Peak District – Dark Peak area

STARTING POINT Snake Inn (GR 112906)

PARKING At the Snake Inn (for patrons only)

PUBLIC TRANSPORT Buses from Glossop and Sheffield

The comparatively little-visited northern edges of Kinder Scout offer one of the best upland promenades in the Dark Peak – a kaleidoscope of constantly changing views, dramatic gritstone tors and a sense of being on top of the world. Starting from the famous landmark of the Snake Inn, this challenging route explores the Edge and descends by the long-established cross-Kinder route which is known as the Snake Path.

■ The Snake Pass (A57) is a major east-west crossing of the Pennines, famous from wintertime weather reports on national radio and television as being usually one of the first routes to close and last to re-open after winter snows. It rises to 1680 ft (512 m) at the Snake Summit, making it one of the highest major roads in Britain.

The pass takes its name from the coaching inn built in 1821, which in turn took its name from the snake that appears in the coat of arms of the Cavendish family (the Dukes of Devonshire), major landowners in these parts. The original turnpike road was constructed under an Act of Parliament of 1818 and was said to be one of the last projects undertaken by the engineer Thomas Telford. It opened in 1821.

▶ From the Snake Inn, turn left and walk (carefully) down the busy A57 to the signposted path through a thin belt of conifers at the eastern end of Nungrain Brink. This leads to a footbridge over the River Ashop. Bear left here, fording the Fair Brook which leads down from the valley of that name, and then climb steeply uphill into the confines of Gate Side Clough ❶.

Following the line of a dilapidated dry-stone wall up the hill, the path gradually deteriorates to an indistinct trod, with a line of disused grouse shooting butts on the opposite bank of the stream. There is no grouse shooting on Kinder these days as it is under National Trust ownership, but this was once a very important local pastime.

Eventually, the faint path tops out just to the right of Seal Stones, named the 'Sele Stones' in J. Hutchinson's *Tour through the High Peak of Derbyshire* of 1809. This is yet another of the strange outcrops of gritstone tors which ring Kinder's flat and peaty summit plateau. The route now turns due west along Seal Edge ❷ for the start of a glorious 4-mile (6.4-km) promenade along Kinder's northern ramparts.

■ Seal Edge is a good example of a periglacial (edge-of-ice-sheet) environment, and it shows both a free face (that is, a steep face free of rocks) and, below it, a blockfield (an area where rocks and scree have accumulated). Areas where possible corries (circular hollows in the bedrock caused by glaciation) have started to form have also been identified below the edge. The views from Seal Edge over the heather-clad valley of the Fair Brook are spectacular, across to the dense forestry plantations which surround the Snake Inn, with the heights of Bleaklow beyond.

▶ Shortly after passing the gulleys of Middle and Upper Seal Clough, you reach the overhanging climbing crag known as the Chinese Wall, on which routes have such appropriate names as 'Cantonuation' and

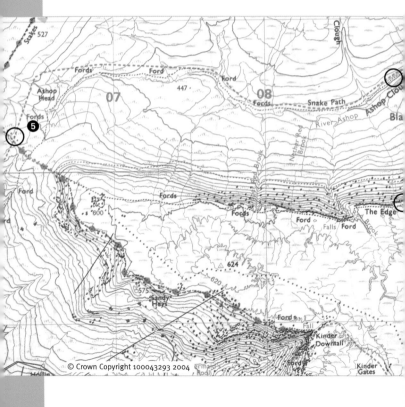

© Crown Copyright 100043293 2004

'Sparkle in the China'. In a few short steps you reach the deep Fair Brook ravine ❸.

If you fancy being with the crowds congregating around Kinder Downfall, it is a short, if strenuous, step south-west from the head of the Fair Brook ravine across the trackless peat haggs and groughs to reach the infant Kinder river near Kinder Gates, which can then be followed down to the Downfall.

The main route swings around the ravine towards Misty Buttresses, where one of the climbing routes is known as 'Magic Wall' because of an undercut buttress which is propped up by an impossibly

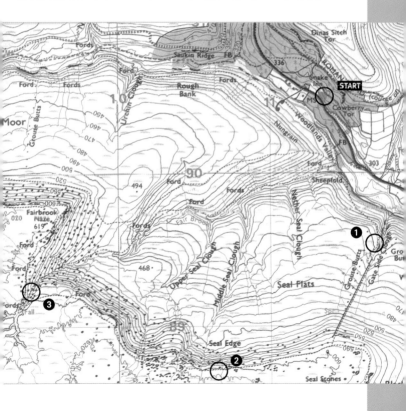

tiny pedestal. There is also a small cave below Egg Crag, another of the Misty Buttresses. Any climbers here are likely to be of the 'old school', because a 4-mile (6.4-km) walk to the climbing is apparently too much for many of today's rock athletes.

The route now goes out on to the spectacular promontory of Fairbrook Naze (*naze* is 'nose' in Old English). Again, the view from here is wonderful, north towards the bogs of Featherbed Moss ('featherbed' does not refer to an easy resting place, but to the common fluffy fruiting heads of cotton grass), brooding Bleaklow across the Snake and south to the long line of Derwent Edge. The heather in the Fair Brook valley beneath is some of the finest in the Peak, and a glorious sight in late summer.

Turn due west again, keeping for convenience to the edge path, along the long line of Ashop Edge, marked on the map simply as The Edge ❹ – and nothing to do with the lead singer of the Irish supergroup U2. After about a mile (1.6 km) of quite rough going on the peaty path, you come to the bizarre tor known,

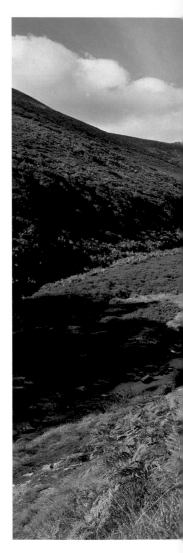

Fair Brook

for obvious reasons, as the Boxing Glove Stones.

Continue on the path, crossing streams named successively the Nether and Upper Red Brooks, which flow down into the valley of the River Ashop. You may notice the scattered remains of a couple of aircraft wrecks on the slopes of the clough below you. From here until you reach its westernmost extremity at Ashop Head, the Edge becomes increasingly more indistinct.

At Ashop Head ❺, you reach the Pennine Way. Descend to the crossroads of the Snake Path coming up from Hayfield (see Walk 3) and the Pennine Way via the award-winning, beautifully constructed staircase built by the National Trust.

Turn right at the prominent junction, and descend on the well-defined Snake Path.

■ The Snake Path was one of the first rights of way to be negotiated over Kinder Scout after the enclosures had made what was once common land into private property. It was only after years of patient negotiation by the Hayfield and Kinder Scout Ancient Footpaths Association and the Peak District and Northern Counties Footpath Society with the landowners, including the Duke of Devonshire, that the 6-mile (9.6-km) path between Hayfield and the Snake Inn was eventually opened to the public, on 29 May 1897.

▶ The Snake Path is now followed eastwards for 3 miles (4.8 km) as it tracks Ashop Clough ❻ on its northern bank, winding through peat haggs and across streams, and passing a ruined shooting cabin about halfway down. The valley narrows towards the bottom end where the prominent Urchin Clough can be seen coming down from Kinder on the opposite bank.

Entering the dense conifers of the Lady Clough plantations under Saukin Ridge, the path finally descends to cross a footbridge and climb up again to the A57 Snake Road. Turning right, from here it is a short way, taking care to avoid the busy traffic, back to the Snake Inn.

Glorious grouse

The sudden cackling 'Go back, go back, g'back, g'back' call of the red grouse is the sound you are most likely to hear when crossing the heather moorlands of the Peak District.

And it is this plump, furry-footed game bird we largely have to thank for the glorious expanse of heather which is such a delight to the eyes and senses in late summer. Especially in the more recent past, the heather moors have been almost exclusively managed to support the red grouse – the nearest thing we have

One half of a brace of grouse

to a uniquely British bird species, although it is now thought to be a sub-species of the European willow grouse.

The red grouse (*Lapogus lapogus*) relies almost entirely on heather for its livelihood. It needs healthy young heather as it eats the fresh shoots (along with copious numbers of crane flies), and it also requires older, woody heather for cover and nesting. Heather is also, of course, valuable food for the sheep with which the grouse shares its home.

To achieve this range of differently aged heather, moorland managers regularly burn or 'swale' the moors in the early spring when the risk of uncontrolled fires is less. It is this swaling which gives the moors their patchwork-quilt appearance, with newly burned areas appearing bare alongside areas where new growth is taking place or where the bushy patches of older heather can be found.

Everything on a grouse moor revolves around the 'Glorious Twelfth' of August, which is when the grouse-shooting season begins. Teams of beaters go out in front of the guns to raise the grouse and drive them over the low stone or turf shooting butts, which, alongside the now often ruinous shooters' cabins such as the one seen on the Snake Path, are common features of a grouse moor.

Sportsmen come from all over the world and pay high prices to shoot Peak District grouse, although disease has limited the number of moors which have been shot in recent years. Some of the 'bags' recorded in the past were truly astonishing. A record was established on the Broomhead Moors in August 1913, when 1421½ brace (2843 birds) were shot in one day.

WALK 6

THE HILL OF THE WINNERS – WIN HILL

DIFFICULTY 🥾 🥾 🥾 **DISTANCE 7 miles (11 km)**

HOPE — TWITCHELL FARM — WIN HILL SUMMIT — HOPE BRINK — WOOLER KNOLL — HOPE CROSS — HOPE

MAP OS Explorer OL1, The Peak District – Dark Peak area

STARTING POINT Hope (GR 172835)

PARKING In the car park at Hope

PUBLIC TRANSPORT Trains run from Stockport and Sheffield to Hope station, ½ mile (0.8 km) east of the village. Buses run from Sheffield.

Although the village of Hope is today overshadowed by its western neighbour, Castleton, its former importance is witnessed by the fact that it gave its name to the whole valley. Hope is overlooked by the long whaleback of Win Hill, one of the finest viewpoints in the Peak, and this easy half-day walk is extended along a haunted Roman road, now in open access, to the ancient landmark of Hope Cross, which is another fine viewpoint.

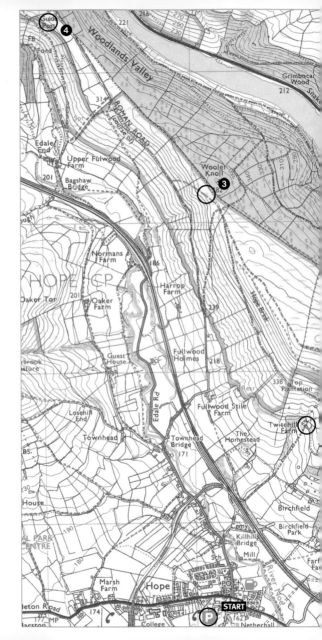

© Crown Copyright 1000/43293 2004

■ Hope is today perhaps best known for its huge cement works – still referred to locally as Earle's but now operated by the Lafarge company – to the south of the village. Carefully screened by landscaping and tree planting, the works is an important source of employment in the Hope valley, and a good example of how a potentially harmful extractive industry can be sympathetically incorporated within a National Park.

Hope's parish church of St Peter dates mainly from the thirteenth and fourteenth centuries but has the shaft of a Saxon preaching cross outside its porch. In 1068, its extensive parish took up two-thirds of the Royal Forest of the Peak (see page 93), and included Buxton, Tideswell and Chapel-en-le-Frith. Hope has a weekly livestock market, first granted in 1715, and a famous agricultural show and sheepdog trials in August, which attract farmers and their families from all over the Peak and from further afield.

▶ From the centre of the village go down the Edale Road opposite the church, beside the Woodruffe Arms. After about ¼ mile (0.4 km), turn right and descend a lane to Killhill Bridge which crosses the River Noe. After passing under the railway bridge, turn right on to a track which ascends towards Twitchell Farm **1**.

Passing the farm buildings, the route now climbs up steep grassy pastures to a stile, from where a clear path bears to the right and mounts ever more steeply by a series of zigzags up Thornhill Brink towards the skyline. Turn right at the top, and climb up on a clear sandy path which winds through the heather towards the obvious summit crags of Win Hill Pike **2**.

■ There are many legends which concern the naming of the hill, the most common of which is that the eventual victors in a Dark Age battle camped here – hence 'Win' Hill – while the losers chose 'Lose' Hill, across the valley of the Noe (see page 94).

The central position of Win Hill in the Peak District ensures that the views from its summit at 1518 ft (462 m) are extensive. To the north, the upper Derwent valley lies across the twin arms of the Ladybower reservoir, with the view stretching towards Derwent Edge and Bleaklow. To the west, Mam Tor stands proudly at the end of the Great Ridge, which runs up from the conical Lose Hill, with Kinder Scout and Brown Knoll in the background. To the south, the view extends across the Hope valley to Shatton Moor with its tall television mast and Bradwell Edge, and beyond to the White Peak limestone plateau.

The Sheffield poet Ebenezer Elliott, the so-called Corn Law Rhymer, composed one of his more effusive descriptive poems in 1876 on experiencing a summer storm on Win Hill. The following are excerpts from Elliott's 'Win-Hill; or The Curse of God':

King of the Peak! Win Hill!
thou, throned and
crown'd,
That reign'st o'er many a
stream and many a vale!
Star-loved, and meteor-
sought, and tempest-
found!
Proud centre of a mountain-
circle, hail!

And this was his view from
the summit:

High on the topmost jewel
of thy crown,
Win-Hill! I sit bareheaded,
ankle-deep
In tufts of rose-cupp'd
bilberries; and look down
On towns that smoke below,
and homes that creep
Into the silvery clouds,
which far-off keep
Their sultry state! And many
a mountain stream,
And many a mountain vale,
'and ridgy steep';
The Peak, and all his
mountains, where
they gleam
Or frown, remote or near,
more distant than they
seem!

▶ After you have admired and
perhaps compared your view with
Elliott's breathless lines, retrace
your steps down to the col of
Thornhill Brink. Continue north
over newly won access land, most
easily on the broad track which
gradually descends the ridge of
Hope Brink, with views towards
Lose Hill across the Noe valley.
Keep to the track which follows
a wall towards Wooler Knoll ❸
on the edge of the conifers of
Wiseman Hey Clough Plantation.

■ The name of Wooler Knoll is
thought to come from the Old
English *wulf hlaw*, meaning
'wolves hill', and its 1253-ft
(382-m) summit (no access) is
now submerged beneath the
dark conifers of Wiseman Hey
Clough Plantation.

This track is marked on the
map as a Roman road. Ghosts
of Roman legionaries have
allegedly been seen marching
up the road from their fort
at Navio near Brough to
Melandra, which guarded the
entrance to Longdendale near
modern Glossop, across the
Snake Pass via Doctor's Gate
(see Walk 1).

▶ page 92

The way to Win Hill Pike

▶ Just past Wooler Knoll, the ridge narrows as it runs down to the ancient, four-square gritstone guidepost of Hope Cross ❹.

■ Hope Cross may originally have been a boundary marker of the Royal Forest of the Peak (see opposite), but it was later adapted to be a guide stoop on the packhorse route between Sheffield and Glossop. The names of these two towns on either side of the Pennines can be seen carved in the capstone of the cross, which also carries the date 1737, probably when the original medieval cross was restored or replaced.

▶ Retrace your steps along the Roman road, keeping to the wall, for about a mile (1.6 km). There are good views from this pleasant track across the Noe valley to the green slopes of Lose Hill. Only the clatter of diesel trains threading the valley below breaks the tranquillity of the scene.

■ The Hope valley line, which is now known as the 'Ramblers' Route', opened to passengers in 1894. It involved the construction of the Cowburn and Totley Tunnels, the latter of which was one of the longest in Britain, measuring 3 miles, 950 yards (5.7 km). Some 700 navvies worked on the line, and 30 million bricks were used to line the tunnel, from which 2.5 million gallons of water had to be extracted daily. Today, the line still provides a spectacular link across the Pennines between Sheffield and Stockport.

▶ The bridleway joins the walled lane which leads down to Fullwood Stile Farm and on through a stile to a path heading south past The Homestead, above to the left. Passing under the railway you are soon back to Killhill Bridge, and left along the Edale Road into Hope.

Royal Forest of the Peak

Soon after the Norman Conquest much of the northern Peak area was taken over as a forty-square-mile (hundred-square-kilometre) royal hunting preserve, the Royal Forest of the Peak. In the early twelfth century, the Longdendale area was added and the forest was divided into three wards: Longdendale in the north, Hopedale in the east and Campana in the south and west. At its greatest extent, the Royal Forest of the Peak stretched from the River Etherow in the north to the Derwent and Tideswell in the east, the Wye in the south and the Goyt in the west.

Like all royal forests, the Peak forest had its own laws and officials, two of whom may have been buried in Hope church. When the chancel was rebuilt in 1881, two thirteenth-century grave slabs were discovered marked with foresters' tools such as the hunting horn, sword and arrow. The Woodruffe Arms in the village may also recall a family of wood reeves (forest officials).

The forest was administered from William Peveril's castle high above Castleton, and there was a foresters' hall or chamber in the centre of the forest at the site of the present-day village which still takes the name of Peak Forest. Forest courts or 'eyres' were held at Bowden, near Chapel-en-le-Frith ('the chapel in the forest'), Tideswell and Castleton or Hope.

Offenders could be arrested for crimes such as 'bloody hand' (if their hands were found to be covered in the blood of a freshly killed deer) or 'back-bear' (carrying a dead deer on their shoulders). Punishments varied from imprisonment to the disabling of hunting dogs by 'lawing' – or cutting off their claws.

Forest laws were relaxed in the mid-thirteenth century, and gradually fell out of use. A fence was built around the forest chamber at Peak Forest in 1579 in a final attempt to protect it, but by the latter half of the seventeenth century the Royal Forest of the Peak had virtually ceased to exist.

The Battle of Win Hill

There are many myths and legends associated with the hills and valleys of the Peak District, and one of the most persistent is about the Battle of Win Hill, said to have taken place at some time in the so-called Dark Ages of the seventh century.

The story is that the battle was fought between the forces of Cuicholm, King of Wessex, and Edwin, King of Northumbria, who had become embroiled in a dispute over boundaries. Cuicholm sent a spy to the court of Edwin with instructions to murder the king. However, the plot was foiled by the heroic intervention of Lilla, one of Edwin's chief thanes, who died as a result of his wounds and who is still commemorated by Lilla Cross, high on the eastern slopes of the North York Moors.

Intent on revenge, Edwin marched south and reached the Peak District, then known as the Land of the Pecsaetan, where Cuicholm had amassed a huge army swelled by the forces of Penda, King of Mercia, another implacable enemy of Edwin.

The opposing armies camped overnight on the twin sentinels of Win Hill and Lose Hill, which effectively guard the entrance to the Edale valley. When they clashed on the following day, somewhere near the present Townhead Bridge, the River Noe, as rivers often did in Dark Age battles, was said to have run red with the blood of the fallen warriors.

Local tradition has it that since Edwin's winning forces had camped on 'Win' Hill the night before, while Cuicholm's had chosen 'Lose' Hill, the result may have been a foregone conclusion. Etymologists, however, are less romantic, and tell us that Win Hill gets its name from the 'withies' (an old name for rowans, which incidentally still grow upon it); Lose Hill (pronounced 'loose') means 'the hill of the pig sties'.

WALK 7

WARD'S PIECE AND THE GREAT RIDGE

DIFFICULTY 👢 👢 **DISTANCE 5 miles (8 km)**

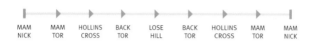

MAM NICK	MAM TOR	HOLLINS CROSS	BACK TOR	LOSE HILL	BACK TOR	HOLLINS CROSS	MAM TOR	MAM NICK

MAP OS Explorer OL1, The Peak District – Dark Peak area

STARTING POINT Mam Nick car park, off the A625 west of Castleton (GR 123832)

PARKING In the car park

PUBLIC TRANSPORT Buses from Chapel-en-le-Frith and Sheffield to Castleton

The shale and grit Mam Tor/Lose Hill ridge stands astride the border of the Dark and White Peaks. It was first named the Great Ridge by the legendary guidebook author and photographer W.A. Poucher, and is now so popular that most of the 2-mile (3-km) route along its crest is paved by gritstone slabs, placed there by the National Trust. The ridge is now completely in open-access land, however, so walkers no longer need to stick to the prescribed track.

▶ The walk starts by ascending the wooden steps which lead up from the back of the Mam Nick car park. Follow the path rising gradually through the trees to emerge at a stile where the Castleton–Edale road passes through the ridge at Mam Nick ('nick' indicates a narrow pass). A crazy-paved staircase of stone leads up the final slopes of Mam Tor to the right, passing through the ramparts which defended the western entrance to the fort ❶.

■ Situated at 1695 ft (517 m) and measuring 16 acres, Mam Tor is one of the highest, largest and most accessible hill forts in the Pennines. The name seems to be Celtic and may mean 'mother mountain', and the bald, windswept summit certainly dominates Castleton and the head of the Hope valley. The much-eroded burial mound, perhaps dating from the Bronze Age, which marks the actual summit has been completely encased in stone cobbles by the National Trust.

Like most hill forts, Mam Tor was originally thought to date from the Iron Age, but excavations by Manchester University found pottery which indicated an earlier, late Bronze Age date for the

substantial double ramparts and the numerous hut circles which dot the interior.

Archaeologists now doubt that such 'forts' had a purely defensive purpose. They may have been used as meeting places or summer sheilings from where stock

could be watched as it grazed the neighbouring hills.

The other popular name for Mam Tor is Shivering Mountain, a reference to the unstable layers of shale and grit which have slipped away from the east face, creating the appearance of a layered cake. In the right weather conditions, hang-gliders and parascenders use Mam Tor as a launch pad, adding more colourful interest to the summit.

The views from Mam Tor are justly famous, extending along the sinuous line of the

Great Ridge to Back Tor and Lose Hill, east down the length of the Hope valley, with Castleton and its castle prominent in the foreground, and west towards the moorland heights of Lord's Seat and Brown Knoll. Kinder Scout and the five 'booths' of Edale in the valley bottom fill the northern view, with Grindslow Knoll prominent above Grindsbrook and the line of the old Pennine Way clearly visible as it winds up the valley.

▶ Take the broad, flagstoned path which leads north through the ramparts of Mam Tor and down to the memorial toposcope (viewpoint stone) at the col of Hollins Cross ❷.

■ This was a stopping place on the 'coffin route' for the deceased of Edale who, before Edale built its own chapel-of-ease and consecrated graveyard in 1633, had to be taken to Castleton for burial. The present Holy Trinity Church in Edale, the spire of which

Mam Tor, the Shivering Mountain

can be seen from the ridge, dates from 1885 and is the third to be constructed in the village.

▶ Now climb up the badly eroded and loose path to the summit of Back Tor ❸, which is a kind of Mam Tor in reverse, for in this case the landslipped face points north-west. It is an impressive, but terribly loose crag with the scruffy remnants of Brockett Booth Plantation climbing its southern slopes.

From Back Tor, the path descends again before the final climb, again on smooth paving slabs, to the conical summit of Lose Hill ❹.

■ The 1563-ft (476-m) summit of Lose (pronounced 'loose') Hill is more properly known as Ward's Piece, in honour of G.H.B. 'Bert' Ward, so-called 'King of the Clarion Ramblers' (see opposite).

The view from Lose Hill looks east across the valley of the Noe to neighbouring Win Hill, and north across Edale to Jagger's Clough and Crookstone Knoll at the eastern end of the Kinder plateau. To the south, Castleton and the glaring white chimney of the Hope Valley Cement Works are the most prominent landmarks, with the rolling White Peak plateau in the background.

▶ Retrace your steps from Lose Hill for a return route of entirely different views of the Dark and White Peaks. Cross Back Tor and Hollins Cross to Mam Tor and then continue back down to the Mam Nick car park.

King of the Clarions

On a blowy April day in 1945, in the presence of a crowd of 2000 ramblers, the summit and fifty-four acres of the eastern side of Lose Hill were presented to G.H.B. 'Bert' Ward by the Sheffield walking community in gratitude for his services to rambling. Typically, he immediately handed the deeds to the National Trust so that, as he said: 'This piece of land will belong to everybody for all times.' Ward would be delighted to know that the summit – now officially known as Ward's Piece – and the surrounding land is today open for all to wander over.

A small advertisement in the socialist paper the *Clarion* had, in late August 1900, invited kindred spirits to join twenty-two-year-old Sheffield engineering fitter Bert Ward on a pioneering walk round Kinder Scout. As a result of the advertisement, a group of eleven men and three women caught the Manchester train from Sheffield, alighting at Edale for a testing circular ramble of about twenty miles (thirty-two kilometres) round the Kinder plateau. They called at the Snake Inn for tea, which

Bert Ward as a young man

consisted of freshly baked bread cakes, boiled ham and tea – all for the princely sum of 1s 3d (about seven pence) each.

Jack Jordan, one of those pioneering Clarionites, later recalled the successful conclusion at Hope Station of that gruelling twelve-hour first walk with the words: 'if our feet were on the heather, our hearts and hopes were with the stars.'

From these modest beginnings was founded one of the earliest and most influential rambling clubs in the north of England – the Sheffield Clarion Ramblers. The fame and fortune of the Clarions were largely down to Ward, who led the club for over fifty years and until his death in 1957 produced, almost single-handedly, the annual editions of the tiny but renowned *Clarion Ramblers' Handbook*, now recognized as gems of outdoor literature.

In addition to quotations from the works of writers about the outdoors such as Henry Thoreau, Ralph Waldo Emerson, Richard Jefferies, John Ruskin and Walt Whitman, the handbooks always included home-spun axioms such as 'A Rambler made is a man improved' and 'The man who never was lost never went very far'.

The advice given for some of the tougher winter rambles advertised in the annual programme did not always avoid falling into misogyny. For example: 'We go, wet or fine, snow or blow, and none but the bravest and fittest must attempt this walk. Those who are unwell, unfit, inexperienced or insufficiently clad should consult their convenience, and that of their friends, by staying at home. Ladies on this occasion are requested not to attend.'

Bert Ward became known as the 'King of the Clarion Ramblers' and was one of the first great campaigners for open access to mountain and moorland. He devoted many articles in the handbooks to what he called 'the gentle art of trespass'. Ward was well known to gamekeepers and landowners and eventually was served with an injunction designed to keep him off part of Kinder Scout for ten years – and 'officially' he never went there during that period.

WALK 8

PARKLANDS OF PEMBERLEY – LYME PARK

DIFFICULTY  **DISTANCE About 5 miles (8 km)**

| LYME PARK | KNOTT | WEST PARKGATE | DALE TOP | STAG HOUSE | BOW STONES | HIGHER MOOR | LYME PARK |

MAP OS Explorer OL1, The Peak District – Dark Peak area

STARTING POINT Lyme Park

PARKING In National Trust car park, Lyme Park (GR 963822). Lyme Park is open between 8 am and 8.30 pm during the summer season.

PUBLIC TRANSPORT Buses from Stockport and Glossop on Sundays and Bank Holidays

Lyme Park, with its classical Palladian façade, is instantly recognizable to lovers of costume drama as Pemberley in the award-winning BBC television adaptation of Jane Austen's *Pride and Prejudice*. Managed by the National Trust and partly financed by Stockport Metropolitan Borough Council, the home of the Legh family for over 550 years stands in a 1400-acre park, which contains the Peak's largest herd of red deer.

■ Lyme Park was designed by the Italian architect Leoni, who transformed the original Tudor house of the Leghs into the present Palladian palace. Interior features include carved woodwork by Grinling Gibbons, Mortlake tapestries and a nationally important collection of English clocks. The 17 acres of gardens include an Edwardian rose garden, a sunken parterre and beautifully maintained herbaceous borders. Lyme Park receives around 400,000 visitors a year, most of whom arrive by car, and with over fifty public events taking place each year, it is a popular playground for the people of Stockport.

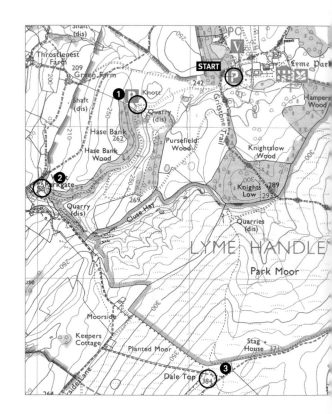

▶ From the car park, take the drive which leads south-west, to the left of what was Mr Darcy's lake in the television drama. As the drive rises gently to a brow, bear right at the fork, heading towards the wall on your right. Now fork left, keeping the small Knott Hill on your left ❶.

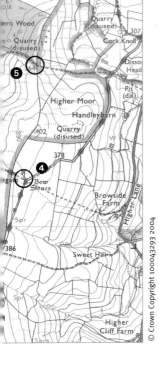

© Crown Copyright 100043293 2004

■ Looking back beyond the house, you will see the prominent early eighteenth-century hunting tower known as Lyme Cage, standing on Cage Hill (no access, except by track). Ahead is a wonderful view across the Cheshire Plain, with the sprawl of industrial Stockport over to the right.

▶ You soon reach a gate where the route becomes a green track under Hase Bank to meet the 9-mile (14.5-km) wall which surrounds the park. Passing through a kissing gate, the track drops to a stile leading to the farm lane to West Parkgate ❷.

Go down the lane to the junction at the Methodist Chapel on the Shrigley Road. Turn left here and climb up the narrow wooded clough known as Cluse Hay to a stile which leads out into the fields again, outside the park wall.

Head uphill towards the isolated cottage of Moorside. Make your way diagonally across the field towards Keeper's Cottage, where a sign points the way uphill again, across Planted

Moor to the summit of Dale Top (1259 ft/384 m) ❸ with fine views back towards the wooded crown of Knights Low, south towards the distant peaks of Shutlingsloe and Shining Tor, and east to the brooding heights of Kinder Scout.

Turn east across Park Moor, following the park wall past Stag House and heading towards the distant top of Bowstonesgate, with the trig point on Sponds Hill (1345 ft/410 m – no access) away to your right.

■ Lyme Park, formerly part of Macclesfield Forest, supports herds of both red and fallow deer, in addition to cattle and sheep which are grazed under licence. The red deer herd is the largest (about 350 head) and probably the oldest (first recorded in 1398) in the Peak District, and if you are here in late autumn at the time of the annual rut, you may well hear the bellowing (correctly known as 'belling') of the mating stags. You might spot these largest of Britain's land mammals

during this walk, or some of the ninety or so more delicate fallow deer.

▶ Follow the boundary wall of the park across the moor. Turn north here, along the now enclosed ridgeway, towards the road end at Bowstonesgate ❹ and Bowstones Farm, with its cluster of television and telephone masts.

■ On the opposite side of the road are the Bow Stones. These are the stumps of two cross shafts which, judging from the traces of carving around their tops, may be of Saxon origin. They were most likely wayside preaching crosses or boundary markers. The local legend, probably based on their name, is that Robin Hood and his men used these stones to string their bows.

In the rough moorland grass near here are a number of Plague Stones, which mark the last resting place of local villagers who died in the Great Plague during the mid-seventeenth century.

▶ Take the ladder stile, which leads back into Lyme Park and towards the house, on the marked Gritstone Way long-distance footpath. You can take a short cut from here back to the house by following the Gritstone Way down across Park Moor and through the trees which cover the 984-ft (300-m) summit of Knights Low.

The main route turns right alongside the park wall, where a pleasant track goes uphill to a memorial viewpoint at the high point of the walk (1319 ft/402 m) on the appropriately named Higher Moor. There is another fine panorama from here, especially looking to the east across to Whaley Bridge with Kinder Scout in the background.

Turn left in front of Lantern Wood ❺, passing between that and Hampers Wood on the left to reach the house again, admiring its setting in the parkland. Walking past the south front and the lake, you will reach a ladder stile which will eventually lead you back to the car park.

Lyme Park

WALK 9

IRON AGE VIEWPOINT – COMBS EDGE

DIFFICULTY 👢 👢 👢 **DISTANCE 5 miles (8 km)**

| COMBS VILLAGE | COMBS EDGE | CASTLE NAZE | COMBS VILLAGE |

MAP OS Explorer OL24, The Peak District – White Peak area

STARTING POINT Beehive Inn, Combs village (GR 041786)

PARKING At the walk start

PUBLIC TRANSPORT Buses run to Chapel-en-le-Frith and trains to Chapel-en-le-Frith station, about a mile (1.6 km) away.

Combs Edge and its neighbouring hill fort of Castle Naze are among the finest viewpoints in the Peak, but were officially out of bounds to walkers until the new access legislation put them both into open country. So this pleasant 5- or 7-mile (8- or 11-km) stroll on the unfashionable western fringe of the National Park can now be freely enjoyed, along with the extensive views it offers over the Goyt valley and beyond into Cheshire.

■ The tiny village of Combs takes its name from the edge which overshadows it – 'comb' or 'coombe' having the same root as the Welsh *cwm*, meaning 'a narrow valley or hollow'. The construction of the Peak

Forest Canal, which was completed in 1797 to serve the limestone quarries at Dove Holes, necessitated the building of the Combs reservoir as a feeder, and it is now the home of a thriving sailing club. The coming of the London and North Western Railway between Buxton and Whaley Bridge in 1863 effectively cut the Combs valley in two.

▶ The walk starts from the road junction opposite the Beehive Inn in Combs village centre. Turn left and follow the minor road, Dyke Lane, which winds around the foot of Combs Edge (ahead) and Castle Naze towards Dove Holes. When you reach Rye Flatt Farm, turn right through the farmyard and walk along the walled lane which heads south.

■ In 1895 Rye Flatt Farm was the home of Herbert Frood, the founder of the gigantic brake-lining company Ferodo (the company's name is a near anagram of his surname), which is based at nearby Chapel-en-le-Frith.

Frood is said to have drawn his fortune-making idea of using industrial belting to slow the wheels of horse-drawn trucks from his father-in-law's Manchester factory.

The farm on the slopes of Combs Moss to your left, Pye Greave, has a connection with Florence Nightingale. In 1840, Florence's father William Nightingale bought Pye Greave, and in later years villagers recalled the two of them riding together on horseback through Combs.

▶ When you reach Allstone Lee Farm on your left ❶, turn to go through the farmyard and out on to a flagged path by the side of a hedge. Bear right as it joins another track which gently contours up the bracken-covered hillside by a series of zigzags, eventually entering a hollow way (an ancient track hollowed out by centuries of use) which takes you steeply up to the plateau edge of Combs Moss at a prominent cleft in the rocky escarpment ❷.

■ According to the botanist Sir A.G. Tansley, 'moss' is

one of the commonest names in the Pennines. It comes from the Old Norse *mosi* meaning 'a bog, swamp or morass', which is a fair description of many of the higher moors in the area, including, in this instance, Combs Moss.

▶ A clear but narrow path leads north-westwards (left) from the top of the climb, running between the boundary wall of the moor and the rocky edge of the escarpment.

If you are feeling particularly energetic, you can choose to follow the infant tributary of Meveril Brook due east towards its source under Black Edge and then continue along this fine ridge walk north to Hob Tor ❸, enjoying the views east across the quarry-scarred landscape of Dove Holes with the White Peak plateau beyond. At Hob Tor turn north-west along Short Edge to reach Castle Naze. This detour would add an extra couple of miles (3 km) to the walk.

The main route takes you on to a sharp promontory which offers outstanding views westwards across the Goyt valley, which is framed by the coniferous plantations of Hoo Moor above the Fernilee reservoir, as well as northwards along the escarpment of Combs Edge to the next craggy promontory, which is capped by the ancient hill fort of Castle Naze.

Follow the promontory round to the next cleft in the trees of the valley below, through which Pyegreave Brook descends towards Pye Greave Farm.

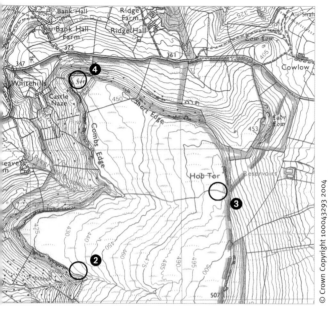

© Crown Copyright 100043293 2004

■ There is a fine view from here down the valley towards the glittering waters of the 80-acre Combs reservoir, built in 1794 as a feeder for the Peak Forest Canal. The reservoir is usually dotted with the white sails of the local sailing club. Northwards, the view takes in the prominent hills of Chinley Churn and South Head, with the ramparts of Kinder Scout looming in the background.

▶ Climbing out of the ravine of the Pyegreave Brook, head north on the glorious promenade along Combs Edge towards the beckoning ramparts of the Castle Naze hill fort ❹.

■ Castle Naze is unusual among the Peak District's eight hill forts, built perhaps 3000 years ago during the late Bronze Age and the Iron Age, in that it has a double rampart. This is typical of a

▶ page 114

Combs Edge

promontory hill fort, a type of construction perhaps better known in Ireland and in Pembrokeshire, where it was often built on coastal cliffs. In this case, the steep crags – a popular playground for rock climbers – to the west and north of Castle Naze made perfect natural defences on those sides.

▶ Cross the moorland wall at its angle beyond the fort, and descend steeply through a rocky gulley and over a couple of stiles to cross the minor road (Dyke Lane) and continue down the broad, grassy access track which leads to Bank Hall Farm. Just beyond the farm buildings a path leads off right downhill towards the railway line and back into Combs. If you are catching a train, follow the path which runs parallel to the railway line and contours around the hill to the house marked on the map as 'Lodge' and the footbridge at the station in Chapel-en-le-Frith.

WALK 10

IN AND OUT OF THE GOYT

DIFFICULTY 👢 👢 👢 👢 **DISTANCE 12 miles (19 km)**

(Shorter alternative 8 miles/13 km)

ERRWOOD   PYM CHAIR   SHINING   BURBAGE   CROMFORD   ERRWOOD
                      TOR   EDGE   & HIGH
    SPANISH   CATS   WILD   PEAK BUNSAL
    SHRINE   TOR   CAT &   MOOR RAILWAY COB
                     FIDDLE
                     INN

MAP OS Explorer OL24, The Peak District – White Peak area

STARTING POINT Errwood

PARKING In car park at Errwood (GR 012748). Note that the road between The Street and Derbyshire Bridge is closed to through traffic on summer weekends.

PUBLIC TRANSPORT Buses from Buxton and Stockport

For many years, the moors surrounding the Goyt valley were the missing link in the Peak District National Park's exemplary portfolio of open-access land. Access agreements were never made with landowners, and so the moors remained frustratingly out of bounds to the walker. The new access legislation has now opened up for the first time the wastes of Wild Moor and Goyt's Moss, which are explored in this quite strenuous moorland walk.

▶ page 118

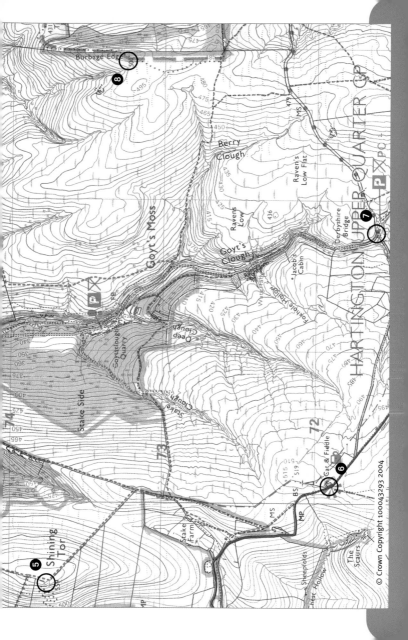

▶ The walk starts from the Forestry Commission car park on the western side of the Errwood reservoir.

■ Errwood reservoir, which covers 78 acres and when full contains 927 million gallons of water, was completed in 1968 to supply water to Stockport. It followed the slightly larger Fernilee reservoir, lower down the valley, which was completed thirty years before. The construction of the Fernilee dam saw the demolition of the hamlet of Goyt's Bridge and the partial destruction of stately Errwood Hall.

Errwood reservoir is now home to a thriving sailing club, whose clubhouse is on the opposite shore of the reservoir from the car park. It is also fished by anglers.

▶ Take the signed Forestry Commission nature trail, which climbs up from the back of the car park to meet the plantations at a gap in the wall. Crossing a stream, you soon come to the romantic and restored ruins of Errwood Hall ❶.

■ Errwood Hall was built in 1830 by Manchester businessman Samuel Grimshawe as a wedding present for his son (see page 125). The Grimshawes lived in this splendid country mansion 'in the style of foreign princes', according to a contemporary account. Their extensive estate was planted with rhododendron and azalea bushes and the woods at the back of the car park are still ablaze with flowers in the early summer.

▶ Continue on the woodland walk up along Foxlow Edge. The Grimshawes' burial ground is away to the left and it is worth the short detour to look at the graves, which include those of Captain John Butler, captain of the Grimshawes' yacht *Marquita*, and many members of the Grimshawe family and their staff. Contour up through the thinning trees to the small, circular building just off the main path. This is known as the Spanish Shrine ❷.

■ This isolated building was erected by the Grimshawe family in 1889 as a memorial to their much-loved governess, Dolores de Bergrin. The daughter of a Spanish aristocrat, Dolores had died in her early forties. The shrine is dedicated to St Joseph and features a beautiful altar with a constantly renewed supply of flowers, backed by a colourful mosaic.

▶ Continue up the steep path across Withinleach Moor to meet the road, which is known simply as The Street. This is an ancient way which may have been a Roman road from the west into Buxton, and was certainly later used as a route by salters bringing the precious commodity from Cheshire into the Peak District. Turn left at the road to climb steadily up to its summit at Pym Chair ❸.

■ Nothing remains now of the landmark on The Street

which was known as Pym Chair. It may have been named after John Pym, the seventeenth-century Puritan and Parliamentarian leader, like the tor of the same name on Kinder's southern edge. There are fine views westwards from here across the Cheshire Plain towards wooded Alderley Edge, and beyond that to the dim hills of Wales. Eastwards, across the deep valley of the Goyt, Combs Moss fills the horizon.

▶ Turn left here and follow the reconstructed moorland path beside the wall, which soon dips to Oldgate Nick, where the hollow ways of numerous former packhorse trails cross the ridge. The path leads steadily upward to the 1703-ft (519-m) summit of Cats Tor – apparently named after the wild cats which once haunted this spot ❹.

The route now dips again down to the col known as the Tors and then climbs steadily to the high point of the walk, Shining Tor (1834 ft/559 m) ❺, which is reached by crossing the wall by a ladder stile.

▶ page 122

Errwood reservoir

■ Shining Tor (GR 994737) is the highest point in Cheshire and the view from its summit is extensive. To the south, it takes in the conifers of Macclesfield Forest, watched over by the conical summit of Shutlingsloe. The great white saucer of the Jodrell Bank radio telescope can usually be seen on the broad Cheshire Plain to the west. Our next point of call, the isolated building of the Cat and Fiddle Inn on the main Buxton to Macclesfield road, is below the tall radio mast.

Shining Tor is a popular venue for hang-gliders, and if the weather and wind conditions are right, several will usually be seen swooping from the top.

▶ Follow the wall south-east down into the boggy col between the head of Shooter's Clough, leading left into the Goyt, and Clough Brook, which flows south towards Macclesfield Forest. Just beyond the col, a path leads up from Shooter's Clough south towards the old Buxton to Macclesfield turnpike road, which joins the modern A57 north of the Cat and Fiddle Inn ❻.

■ Standing at 1690 ft (515 m), the Cat and Fiddle Inn is the second-highest hostelry in England, and a welcome landmark to travellers on the A57, especially in winter. (Incidentally, it is the Tan Hill Inn above Swaledale in the Yorkshire Dales that is the highest pub in England, at 1732 ft/528 m.) The Cat and Fiddle Inn was built in the early nineteenth century by banker John Ryle of Macclesfield, who also purchased the entire Errwood estate. There are many theories as to how it got its intriguing name, but the carved stone plaque at the front of the inn, which shows a grinning cat playing a fiddle, seems to indicate that it is associated with the children's nursery rhyme, 'Hey, Diddle Diddle'. This is a good place to stop for refreshments, about halfway round the walk.

▶ A few hundred yards (metres) south of the Cat and Fiddle, the minor road to Derbyshire Bridge branches off the A57, heading down towards the defile of Goyt's Clough and the infant River Goyt. Follow this road to Derbyshire Bridge ❼, now a Ranger Service briefing point, with public toilets.

A shorter alternative is to follow the minor road which leads down into the confines of Goyt's Clough. This pleasant road passes a reconstructed packhorse bridge from the drowned hamlet of Goyt's Bridge and a quarry, on the left, which was the birthplace of the Pickford's removals empire, before leading back to the Errwood car park in about 2 miles (3 km).

The main moorland route now follows the walled track, which again heads along the line of the old Buxton to Macclesfield turnpike, leading eastward over Raven's Low Flat, passing Berry Clough on your left. At spot height 479 on the map, a path leads right (north) over the eastern slopes of Berry Clough and on to the open moor, which is ablaze with a glorious display of heather in late summer.

When the path bends to the left, leave it and head north-east across the rough tussock grass and heather moorland towards the high point (1640 ft/500 m) of the ridge of Burbage Edge ❽. There are great views east from here across the wall towards Buxton, showing this spa town's fine setting in the heart of the hills. You should be able to pick out the dome of the Royal Hospital (now part of the University of Derby) and the enormous Palace Hotel.

Still heading north across the aptly named Wild Moor, the well-worn track heads for the depression at the head of Wildmoorstone Brook, which is the cutting used by the former Cromford and High Peak Railway as it emerged from the north portal of Burbage Tunnel under the moors. The line of the old railway is now followed over two embankments, crossing the valley of the Wildmoorstone Brook and contouring across the moor to meet metalled Goyt's Lane by a small reservoir and car park ❾.

■ Originally designed as a canal (its stations were called wharfs), the 32-mile (52-km) single-track Cromford and High Peak Railway was built at the very start of the railway age. Constructed by Josiah Jessop and opened in 1830, it was designed to link the Peak Forest Canal at Whaley Bridge with the Cromford Canal, south of Matlock. It was not a success, and passenger services were withdrawn in 1877 after a fatal accident. The line finally closed in 1967. The reservoir near the car park on Goyt's Lane provided water for one of the stationary steam engines used to regulate the hauling of trains up the steep Bunsal Cob incline.

▶ Turn left at Goyt's Lane and descend the railway incline down to the car park and toilets at Bunsal Cob 🔟, where a plaque was erected in 1972 by the Stephenson Locomotive Society. It incorporates one of the original stone sleepers and records the use of the old railway inclines to construct the Errwood dam.

■ Using an ingenious compensatory system, three loaded wagons going down the Bunsal incline pulled six empty ones up, with the stationary steam engine acting as a regulator to check their progress. Before the arrival of steam locomotives, trucks were hauled along level sections of the line by horses.

▶ It is now a simple case of following the road over the dam wall of the Errwood reservoir and continuing round to the left over the Shooter's Clough bridge and back to the Errwood car park.

The Grimshawe Empire

Visitors to the picturesque Goyt valley are usually fascinated by the ruins of Errwood Hall, now restored and hidden among the trees above the Errwood reservoir.

This was the grand, Italianate mansion of the Grimshawes, a Manchester family which had made its wealth from merchandizing. Under Samuel Grimshawe they moved to their new mansion in the Goyt valley in 1830 and dominated the valley and its life for the next century.

The house was designed by the amateur architect Alexander Beresford Hope of Staffordshire as a turreted, double-winged country house with a central tower in the then fashionable classical Italian style. The family lived and entertained at Errwood in great style, especially during the grouse-shooting season on the adjoining moors, when many titled guests would stay. The Grimshawes were also great travellers with their own ocean-going yacht named the *Marquita*, in which they travelled the world and brought back some of the 40,000 rhododendron and azalea shrubs which were planted in the grounds, and which today have gone wild and give such a marvellous show in the spring.

It was said that to stand in the tower of the hall and admire the view across the valley at rhododendron-time was a wonderful experience. According to an old guidebook, 'The beauty of the blooms gave the impression that a rainbow had moved across and left its colours behind.'

Errwood Hall's heyday lasted until 1930, when Stockport Corporation bought the estate to build the Fernilee reservoir, and for a short while the hall was used as a youth hostel. But the building was dismantled in 1934 in the interests of water purity, along with thirteen farms and cottages which once formed the Grimshawe estate. The Errwood reservoir, named after the hall, followed in 1968, when it was opened by the Duchess of Kent.

WALK 11

CHESHIRE'S MATTERHORN –
SHUTLINGSLOE

DIFFICULTY 👢 👢 👢   **DISTANCE 6 miles (10 km)**

| TRENTABANK RESERVOIR | SHUTLING-SLOE | WILDBOAR-CLOUGH | GREENWAY BRIDGE | OAKEN CLOUGH | HARDINGS FARM | TRENTABANK RESERVOIR |

MAP OS Explorer OL24, The Peak District – White Peak area

STARTING POINT Trentabank car park, on the minor road to Macclesfield Forest east of Langley (GR 961711)

PARKING In Trentabank car park

PUBLIC TRANSPORT Occasional buses from Macclesfield

Shapely Shutlingsloe – one of very few peaks in the Peak District to merit the name – is sometimes known as the 'Matterhorn of Cheshire', although the ridge only seems like that when seen from the north or the south. This walk starts from the conifers of Macclesfield Forest and takes in the village of Wildboarclough.

■ Trentabank reservoir was constructed in 1929 to supply drinking water to Macclesfield and district, and is now managed by United Utilities. The log cabin-style visitor and ranger briefing centre is run by the National Park and by the water company in partnership.

The authorities have also constructed an excellent nature trail suitable for disabled people, which runs down to the reservoir.

Trentabank reservoir and the surrounding forest area support a wide variety of wildlife, most spectacular of which is the large heronry on the island visible from the roadside. The heronry is managed by the Cheshire Wildlife Trust, and in addition to the herons, red-breasted merganser, great crested grebe and goldeneye can also be seen on the reservoir.

▶ From the visitor centre turn right on the concessionary path which runs beside the road, and follow it as it becomes a track climbing steeply through the conifers of Macclesfield Forest to emerge on to the open moor.

■ Coniferous forests are not always conducive to wildlife, but Macclesfield Forest boasts a herd of fallow deer as well as foxes, badgers, tawny owls, goldcrests, woodpeckers and finches.

On the moor above, birds of prey including buzzard and kestrel can be regularly seen.

▶ The track becomes a paved causeway as it crosses High Moor, with Shutlingsloe towering ahead. The paving was laid by Cheshire County Council and the Peak District National Park in 1992 to overcome severe erosion on the path in the stretch crossing the peaty ground of High Moor. A helicopter was used to transport the recycled slabs which, like those used on the Pennine Way across Kinder and Bleaklow, had been taken from derelict cotton mills.

The path follows a wall to a ladder stile just before the last, steep climb up to the ridgetop summit of Shutlingsloe ❶, through a staircase of outcropping sandstone crags.

■ Shutlingsloe derived its unusual name from an early settler called Scyttel – it means 'Scyttel's Hill'. The craggy summit, which has a memorial toposcope, provides the setting for the exciting denouement to Alan

Garner's classic children's fantasy story, *The Weirdstone of Brisingamen*.

At 1660 ft (506 m), the summit of Shutlingsloe offers some of the finest views in the Peak, extending eastwards across the wooded valley of Wildboarclough to Axe Edge and Oliver Hill, and north towards Shining Tor and distant Kinder Scout. To the south, the rocky escarpments of the Roaches and Ramshaw Rocks and the tall radio mast at Sutton Common can be seen, while the broad Cheshire Plain with Macclesfield in the foreground fills the western view. On a clear day, the saucer-like dish of the Jodrell Bank radio telescope can also be seen.

▶ A waymark on the summit points down to Wildboarclough. After a steep scramble, the path emerges at a stile above Shutlingsloe Farm, which is passed to the left. The route then joins the farm drive and follows it down to the lane which

© Crown Copyright 100043293 2004

leads right and drops down to the road into Wildboarclough **2**.

■ The original name of Wildboarclough was Crag, and this is recalled in the Crag Inn, a popular hostelry passed on the route. Wildboarclough's other claim to fame, apart from the mineral water produced in its name, is its former Post Office, which was one of the largest village post offices in the country.

Crag Mill, now in residential use, is a splendid eighteenth-century Georgian building which was formerly the mill manager's house and administration block. Crag Mill spun silk for the Great Exhibition held at Joseph Paxton's Crystal Palace in 1851. The little parish church of St Saviour dates from the early years of the last century.

▶ From the car park of Crag Inn at the southern end of the village, take a stile on your right and follow the path which contours around the gorse-dotted slopes of Mount Pleasant,

between Higher Nabbs Farm on the right and Lower Nabbs Farm below to the left, to reach the road again just below Greenway Bridge **3**.

Just before reaching Greenway Bridge, turn right at a stile and follow the banks of

Highmoor Brook to cross it by a slab bridge.

It is possible under new open-access rights to take a short cut almost due north from here, following the line of the Highmoor Brook up and across Piggford Moor, Sheepclough Gutter and High Moor, to reach the conifers of Macclesfield Forest direct at Nesset Hill. But it is rough going and most people will probably take the easier, lower option to Oaken Clough and the refreshment offered by the Hanging Gate public house.

Shutlingsloe

At a ruined hut, you will find a concessionary path that goes around Oakenclough House and through new plantations to join the house drive. Bear right to meet a stile which leads left across High Moor between a cluster of peaty tarns, with views back to Shutlingsloe.

Follow this path to the corner of the moor and a stile which leads down on a walled path to emerge on the road at the Hanging Gate public house ❹.

■ The Hanging Gate has a rather brusque sign, which reads:

This gate hangs here
And troubles none
Refresh and pay
And travel on.

▶ Turn right and keep right at a sharp hairpin bend in the main road past Brownlow Farm, Hardings Farm and the delightfully named Thickwithers on the right. Ahead, the prominent neb of Tegg's Nose

peeps over the conifers of Macclesfield Forest.

■ The original Forest of Macclesfield was a hunting ground for wild boar and deer used by Ranulf, Earl of Chester, during the Norman period, and initially it included the Leek and Alstonefield Friths in Staffordshire. The Earl of Chester eventually granted the Staffordshire parts of the forest to the Malbanc family, after which they were known as Malbanc Frith. Macclesfield Forest reverted to the Crown in the mid-thirteenth century when it became a royal hunting forest, like the Royal Forest of the Peak.

▶ The road gradually descends back into the conifers, where you turn right at a sharp bend above the Ridgegate reservoir, through the trees to the left, to drop down steeply back towards the dam of the Trentabank reservoir and your starting point.

WALK 12

THE ROACHES AND GRADBACH

DIFFICULTY 🥾 🥾 🥾   **DISTANCE About 9 miles (14.5 km)**

HEN CLOUD — THE ROACHES — DOXEY POOL — ROACH END — BACK FOREST RIDGE — LUD'S CHURCH — BACK FOREST — GRADBACH — GRAD-BACH HILL — GOLD-SITCH MOSS — HAZEL BARROW — THE ROACHES

MAP OS Explorer OL24, The Peak District – White Peak area

STARTING POINT Unclassified road north of Upper Hulme (GR 004621)

PARKING There is limited roadside car parking near Rockhall Cottage. The Roaches are served on summer weekends by a park-and-ride service from Tittesworth reservoir.

PUBLIC TRANSPORT Buses run to Tittesworth from Buxton and Leek.

The 'Wild West' of the Peak District is dominated by the syncline (downfold in the rocks) created by the Roaches, Hen Cloud and the Ramshaw Rocks, while Gradbach Hill, just to the north, has been opened up under the new access legislation. This 9-mile (14.5-km) walk also visits the legend-haunted chasm of Lud's Church, in the depths of Back Forest.

▶ From the roadside, follow the broad track which leads up to the col between the Roaches and Hen Cloud, which looks like a miniature inland Rock of Gibraltar to your right.

▶ page 136

133

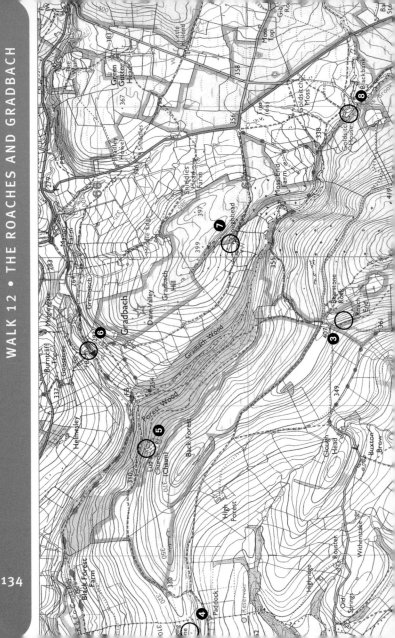

START

© Crown Copyright 1000/43293 2004

■ Tucked away to the left under the overhanging rocks of the Roaches is a cottage partly built into the cliff face known as Rock Hall. It is now a climbers' bothy but was formerly occupied by the eccentric gamekeeper Dougie Moller, the axe-wielding, self-styled 'Lord of the Roaches'.

▶ At the col, turn right on the rough climbers' path which ascends to the shapely 1345-ft (410-m) summit of Hen Cloud (GR 009616) ❶.

■ The name Cloud comes from the Old English *clud* meaning 'rock' or 'hill', but is a name which strangely only seems to be used on the western side of the Peak (for example, the Cloud above Congleton, which is visible at the northern end of the Roaches ridge, and Thorpe Cloud, at the entrance to Dovedale). Hen Cloud stands at the apex of the Roaches syncline and there is a fine view from here looking north across the 'pie dish' of the lower-lying coal measures of

Goldsitch Moss, between the higher ground of the Roaches to the west and Ramshaw Rocks to the east. Gradbach Hill is in the distance.

▶ Turn back and regain the col to ascend the southern end of the Roaches through the rocks, to eventually reach the upper tier of the ridge ❷.

■ The name Roaches simply means rocks, and comes from the Norman French *roches*. This spectacular landscape has attracted attention ever since Dr Robert Plot wrote in 1730 in his *Compleat History of Staffordshire*, 'Here are also vast Rocks which surprise with Admiration, called the Henclouds and Leek Roches. They are of so great a height and afford such stupendous Prospects that one could hardly believe they were anywhere to be found but in Picture.'

The Roaches provide some of the toughest gritstone climbs in the Peak. One such is the overhanging roof route of the Sloth, first climbed by

Don Whillans in 1954 and so-named because of the amount of time the climber spends hanging upside down. The equally descriptive Mincer was first climbed by Joe Brown in 1950.

▶ The route now follows the crest of the Roaches ridge on a superb promenade with extensive views to the left through the impressive rock buttress and across the Staffordshire Plain towards the glinting waters of Tittesworth reservoir. The path gently ascends to the peaty hollow which contains Doxey Pool.

■ Doxey Pool is recorded in the Domesday Book as Dochesig, and may refer to a long-lost personal name. But, like so many other features in the Staffordshire moorlands, it is also linked to a legend. This shallow, peaty pool is said to have neither inlet nor outlet and to be the home of a mermaid, who attracts unwise young men to a watery grave. Other stories tell of a

The Roaches

fearsome green monster known as Jenny Greenteeth, who haunts the murky depths.

▶ From Doxey Pool, the path starts a gradual ascent towards the trig point at Roach End, the summit of the Roaches ridge (1675 ft/505 m), with views north-west, where the shapely cone of Shutlingsloe rises above the valley of the Dane, and due west, to the Cloud above Congleton.

A series of worn steps lead down to the minor road at Roach End ❸. Cross the road and carry on over a ladder stile, which gives on to a path following the dry-stone wall along the top of the un-named ridge above Back Forest, down to your right. This is a wonderful, airy promenade with fine views either side.

After about 1½ miles (2.5 km), just before reaching the Hanging Stone (no access) ❹, a path follows a dry-stone wall off to the right and contours round the hill to descend into the first trees of Back Forest near spot height 310 on the map.

At this point, keep to the upper path which leads through the mixed woodland to the mysterious cleft known as Lud's Church (GR 987656) ❺.

■ Lud's Church is one of the most atmospheric and evocative places in the Peak. Although marked as a cave on the map, it is actually a large, dog-legged landslip 60 ft (18 m) deep, hung with ferns and mosses and usually very damp and muddy underfoot.

Research published in the late 1950s associated Lud's Church with the Green Chapel found in the anonymous, early medieval Arthurian poem *Sir Gawain and the Green Knight*. According to Professor Ralph Elliott of Keele University, Lud Church was where Gawain met up with the fabled knight 'all garbed in green' to perform a Celtic-style beheading ritual. The name of the chasm is said to come from Walter de Lud-Auk, a fourteenth-century Lollard supporter of John Wycliffe, who held services in the cavern, hidden away from the persecution of the authorities.

▶ Having passed through Lud's Church and emerged at the other end, take the sandy path which leads through ancient oak woodland to the gritstone outcrop known as Castle Cliff Rocks. The outcrop overlooks the upper Dane valley, with views to Tagsclough Hill opposite.

Now take the broad track which leads down through the mixed trees of Back Forest to the footbridge over the Black Brook. The route joins the waymarked Dane Valley Way, leading to the hamlet of Gradbach **6** with its fine youth hostel housed in a former cotton mill.

A faint path leaves the road in Gradbach and climbs the northern ridge of Gradbach Hill (GR 001663) to reach its summit at 1309 ft (399 m) and a fine view north towards Shutlingsloe and the Cat and Fiddle Moors above the Goyt valley. Westwards, the view is across the wooded valley of the Black Brook and south towards the Roaches.

Descend southwards to reach the footpath near Cloughhead **7**, turning left into a walled lane and arriving at the road and a crossroads of routes near spot

height 356. Take the footpath which leads due south from here, passing the remains of spoil tips over to your right. These are the remnants of the former bell pits of a short-lived coal-mining industry, which took place on the low-lying Goldsitch Moss in the eighteenth and nineteenth centuries.

The path leads towards the valley of the Black Brook, then follows the stream on its eastern side, joining the walled track which gives access to Goldsitch House **8**. Beyond here, the track heads south past Blackbank and then uphill to join the road, where you turn right and walk up to the junction at Hazel Barrow (spot height 399) **9**.

Turn right again and follow the minor road at the next junction, and turn right again at the next fork. You will soon see a footpath leading off to the left, alongside a wall. With Summerhill to your left, this climbs steadily south between dilapidated walls towards the smooth shape (from this side) of Hen Cloud. You are soon back at the col between the southern end of the Roaches and Hen Cloud, where you rejoin your outward route.

Some further reading

Here is a small selection of books which will tell you more about the area. Please note that not all are still in print.

Anon., *Tom Stephenson*, The Ramblers' Association, n.d.

John Barnatt and Ken Smith, *The Peak District: Landscapes through Time*, Windgather Press, 2004

Rex Bellamy, *The Peak District Companion*, David & Charles, 1981

David Clarke, *Supernatural Peak District*, Robert Hale, 2000

Ron Collier and Roni Wilkinson, *Dark Peak Aircraft Wrecks 1*, Barnsley Chronicle Newspaper Group, 1979; new editions Wharncliffe Publishing, 1990, and Leo Cooper (Pen and Sword Books), 1995–2000

Roger Dalton, Howard Fox and Peter Jones, *Classic Landforms of the Dark Peak*, The Geographical Association, 1999

Luke Garside, *Kinder Scout: the Footpaths and Bridle-Roads about Hayfield*, etc, Hayfield & Kinder Scout Ancient Footpaths Association, 1880

Howard Hill, *Freedom to Roam*, Moorland, 1980

Roy Millward and Adrian Robinson, *The Peak District*, Eyre Methuen, 1975

Hannah Mitchell, *The Hard Way Up*, Faber & Faber, 1968

Mark Richards, *High Peak Walks*, Cicerone, 1982

Benny Rothman, *The 1932 Kinder Trespass*, Willow, 1982

David Sissons (ed.), *The Best of the Sheffield Clarion Ramblers' Handbooks*, Halsgrove, 2002

Roland Smith, *First and Last*, Peak Park Joint Planning Board, 1978

Roly Smith (ed.), *Kinder Scout – Portrait of a Mountain*, Derbyshire County Council, 2002

Roly Smith, *Murder and Mystery in the Peak*, Halsgrove, 2004

Roly Smith, *Peak District: Collins Rambler's Guide*, HarperCollins, 2000

Roly Smith, *The Peak District: Official National Park Guide*, Pevensey (David & Charles), 2000

Brian Stone (trans.), *Sir Gawain and the Green Knight*, Penguin, 1959

The Country Code

An abbreviated version of the Country Code, launched in 2004 and supported by a wide range of countryside organizations including the Ramblers' Association, is given below.

Be safe – plan ahead and follow signs

Even when going out locally, it's best to get the latest information about where and when you can go; for example, your rights to enter some areas of open land may be restricted while work is being carried out, for safety reasons or during breeding seasons. Follow advice and local signs, and be prepared for the unexpected.

Leave gates and property as you find them

Please respect the working life of the countryside, as our actions can affect rural livelihoods, the safety and welfare of animals and people, and the heritage that belongs to all of us.

Protect plants and animals, and take your litter home

We have a responsibility to protect the countryside now and for future generations, so make sure you don't harm animals, birds, plants or trees.

Keep dogs under control

The countryside is a great place to exercise dogs, but it's every owner's duty to make sure their dog is not a danger or nuisance to farm animals, wildlife or other people.

Consider other people

Showing consideration and respect for other people makes the countryside a pleasant environment for everyone, whether they are at home, at work or at leisure.

Index

143

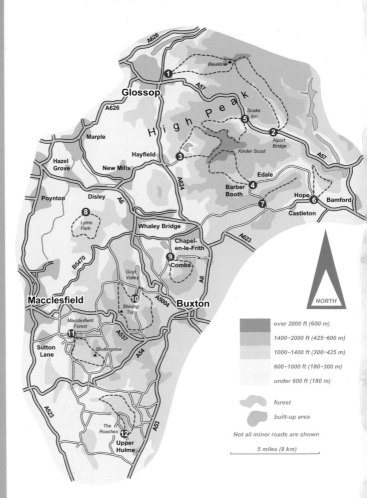

over 2000 ft (600 m)

1400–2000 ft (425–600 m)

1000–1400 ft (300–425 m)

600–1000 ft (180–300 m)

under 600 ft (180 m)

forest

built-up area

Not all minor roads are shown

5 miles (8 km)